"*Disrupting Digital Business* articulates in simple and compelling terms the new business models, customer promises, and transformational mind-sets required to survive and thrive in today's digital world order."

—Clara Shih, founder and CEO, Hearsay Social;
Board Director, Starbucks; and author, *The Facebook Era*

"If you don't have time to read lots of books on the state of the digital frontier of disruption, read this one. It covers everything you need to know, and it will seriously challenge your thinking."

—Annalie Killian, Director of Innovation,
AMP Limited; founder and Executive Producer,
Amplify Festival

"There's no shortage of opinions on the topic of digital disruption, but no one presents the case for change as cohesively as Ray Wang. From establishing authenticity and trust to delivering a brand's promise at every touch point, Ray uses concrete models and real-world examples to break down how innovative organizations thrive in the peer-to-peer economy."

—David Armano, Global Strategy Director,
Edelman Digital

"Ray Wang makes the case for enterprise change that requires new leadership and new thinking. He explains why change is happening increasingly faster, that it's unprecedented to see multiple paradigms shifting concurrently, and why digital is embedded in the DNA of change. Reading this book will help you create change that captures value instead of sitting back and watching value be destroyed."

—Richie Etwaru, Chief Digital Officer, Cegedim

"Leaders in the midst of digital transformation will recognize the challenges represented in these case studies—and gain solid insights on how to manage in a new world of trust and radical transparency."

—Perry Hewitt, Chief Digital Officer,
Harvard University

"Wang provides interesting insights on how to lead through digital disruption and not let it lead you."

—Rachel Botsman, founder, Collaborative Lab;
coauthor, *What's Mine Is Yours: The Rise of
Collaborative Consumption*

DISRUPTING DIGITAL BUSINESS

DISRUPTING DIGITAL BUSINESS

CREATE AN AUTHENTIC EXPERIENCE IN THE PEER-TO-PEER ECONOMY

R "RAY" WANG

HARVARD BUSINESS REVIEW PRESS

BOSTON, MASSACHUSETTS

Copyright 2015 Harvard Business School Publishing Corporation
All rights reserved
Printed in the United States of America

10 9 8 7 6 5 4 3 2 1

The web addresses referenced in this book were live and correct at the time of the book's publication but may be subject to change.

Library-of-Congress Cataloging-in-Publication data is forthcoming
ISBN: 978-1-4221-4201-1
eISBN: 978-1-62527-053-5

The paper used in this publication meets the requirements of the American National Standard for Permanence of Paper for Publications and Documents in Libraries and Archives Z39.48-1992.

CONTENTS

CONTENTS

DISRUPTING DIGITAL BUSINESS

CHAPTER 1

KEEPING THE BRAND PROMISE

We're standing at the dawn of a digital business revolution. As with the beginning of every revolution, those in the midst of it can feel it, sense it, and realize that something big is happening. Yet it's hard to quantify the shift. The data isn't clear. It's hard to measure. The pace of change is accelerating. Old rules seem not to apply. It's hard to put any kind of structure around the changes and to put the pieces together.

But we can *qualify* the shift. We're doing it piecemeal. We have one-off stories about massive business model disruption. And all of us can see the impact digital technology is having on our personal lives. From how we interact with one another to how we engage with organizations, the changes are right in front of us.

This is just the beginning of massive, disruptive, digital transformation. Businesses will fall by the wayside, jobs as we know them will disappear, and competitors will emerge with new value propositions. Digital business will usher in an era of extreme velocity, crystalline transparency, and unforgiving precision.

On the positive side, new models will accelerate the delivery of innovation and drive friction out of business models. New efficiencies will free up resources and time for innovation. Different skill-set requirements will create new types of jobs.

The changes started, of course, when the internet revolution caused bits and pieces of this new world to emerge. We caught a glimpse of it when internet business models disrupted brick and mortar businesses in the 2000s. The recession of 2008 didn't slow the pace of change. In fact, the recession was a catalyst and accelerant. Billions of dollars were poured into new business models, and technology start-ups focused on disrupting existing businesses. In the past decade, we've seen new business models arise from concepts such as social media, cloud computing, video and unified communications, mobility, big data, and the Internet of Things.

These technological concepts have paved the way for the art of the possible. While each trend may have seemed to signify the next big thing, the reality is that none was truly revolutionary on its own. What we've come to realize is that it is the convergence of these technological advances, paired with political, environmental, societal, economic, and legislative shifts, that has formed the basis of the digital business revolution we find ourselves in today.

The companies, brands, enterprises, and organizations that are winning in this digital era are doing so not just because of disruptive technology but also because of a deep understanding of what it takes to build an organization in a digital age and on a digital scale. Successful leaders foster a culture of digital DNA and infuse an understanding of what's required to build new business models with disruptive technology.

In this new world, brand mythology becomes paramount. Your company's brand must stand for something: it must answer the "why" of the firm's existence. But companies need to go beyond telling a simple brand story. Every interaction, every touch point, must reflect the authenticity of the brand's promise. This brand message must resonate consistently throughout the organization at every level. We're at a point where we no longer merely sell products or deliver on services. In the digital world, customers require businesses to focus on delivering authentic experiences and outcomes. We're moving from selling products to keeping brand promises.

Keeping brand promises requires authenticity, because the need for trust and transparency radically increases in a digital world. The reward for authenticity in keeping brand promises can be strong gains. Disney, Fox News, GE, the Mayo Clinic, Philips, Sephora, and Virgin America are examples of companies that show how keeping brand promises sustains margins, grows market share, and improves customer loyalty.

Brands and businesses that fail to deliver on promises may enter a never-ending death match to deliver faster, better, and cheaper. All businesses should shoot for efficiency, but the inability to earn margins will often come at the expense of innovation. Businesses that don't embrace the digital world will lack the products, people, and cachet required to win. Those businesses are forced into survival mode in the fast-moving digital business environment. That's like trying to tread water in a hurricane.

Business leaders working in this new world already recognize that attempts to ignore the seismic shift from business as usual to disruptive digital business models can result in harsh market punishment. Witness the devastation in industries such as retail, media, and publishing, which are seeing significant revenue decline, restructurings, and bankruptcies. Yet, for a select few organizations, the embrace of digital principles has rewarded leaders and their organizations with significant marketplace advantages and business model disruption.

The key to companies' success will be to develop disruptive digital business models of their own. Organizations and individuals will have to know who they want to be—and to live and breathe it. To develop disruptive digital business models, companies must aspire to be:

- **Transformation focused:** Incremental innovation is not enough. Organizations have to design for large-scale, companywide transformational innovation.

- **Relevant:** Context drives the ability to deliver mass personalization at scale.

- **Authentic:** Digital provides trust and radical transparency through massive data backbones and open access.

- **Intention driven:** Best practices rules and processes aren't enough, we have to predict what's expected next.

- **Networked:** New people-to-people (P2P) networked economies are guided by ephemeral self-interest and

the ability to open up the business to co-create and
co-innovate with all types of partners.

Success in developing disruptive digital business models
requires mastery of all five of these areas. While mastery
can't be achieved piecemeal, consider these as the design
points in order to disrupt digital businesses.

Many of today's digital business winners outpace their
market competition exponentially in revenue growth and
overall profitability. Companies such as Amazon, Airbnb,
eSurance, Evernote, Lending Club, Lyft, Nest, Tesla, and
Uber are creating new digital business models. On average,
these category leaders drive 70 percent of the profits and
40 percent of the market share. With that type of growth,
those that fall behind may never recover. Those who do
the disrupting will rewrite history and emerge to be their
category leaders in their own right. Early adopters—the
market leaders and fast followers—are winning.

Disrupting Digital Business should not be seen just as an
analysis of new digital business models and trends. This
book is written for business leaders who seek insights on
how they can serve as a catalyst for change and transform
their business strategy to not only disrupt existing digital
business competitors, but also to create new opportunities

for growth. In fact, companies such as ARI Fleet Services, Avis, GE, Honeywell, Marriott, and Philips are fighting back and turning the tables around. These companies should offer inspiration on how old-line businesses can disrupt digital business.

As you read through the chapters, keep asking these questions: Who is disrupting your business today, and how might nontraditional competitors disrupt your market? The insights offered in this book can help you quickly figure out how to take your company from disrupted to disruptor. The goal—disrupt digital businesses before you get disrupted!

CHAPTER 2

BEING TRUE TO YOURSELF

BUSINESS MODEL TRANSFORMATION

T he heart and soul of disrupting digital business comes from a passion for transformation. This is more than just a drive for incremental improvement or even a special ops team of ninjas or tiger teams. Organizations must build a culture with a transformational mindset. Transformation-minded organizations do more than just challenge the status quo: they try to understand the root cause of the problem. They want to understand the possibilities. They want to push the limits. They want to see how they can take things to the very top. With this mind-set, leaders can borrow new business models from other industries, adjacencies that they wouldn't have seen before. They might also create new business models as they see new types of technologies enter the market.

This transformation will require a pioneering spirit and an organizational culture that's not afraid to innovate. How do we infuse a digital mind-set into the DNA of the entire corporate organism? This transformation is not just needed for sustaining change and fostering a sustainable cycle of innovation, it's critical to the success of an organization. You can try to force this thinking from the top down, but it will only go so far. Your employees must be empowered to move from the bottom up. Research shows that organizations that can deliver transformational innovation not only effectively compete, but they also win disproportionately in the marketplace.

Incremental versus Transformational Innovation

Incremental innovation, once viewed as the key to sustained success, is now the norm. It's expected. And it's just not enough. On the other hand, transformational innovation doesn't necessarily improve on the existing model. It creates breakthroughs. You launch new product categories. You disrupt existing business models. You cannibalize existing businesses. Transformational innovation is hard. It's scary. It's hairy. And most people don't get there, because the culture's not there.

So how do you do it? First you have to understand your organizational DNA. You also have to understand the difference between incremental innovation and transformational innovation. And, more important, you've got to focus in on the business model shifts. This is not about technology. Simply adding a digital moniker in front of a tired concept is not enough. This movement is about breakthrough innovations in business models, and it is a completely different way of looking at things.

Organizational DNA

So let's start by talking about understanding your organizational DNA. The first question to ask is, How ready are you for transformation? If you feel your company is truly ready for change, a systematic approach is to build this culture from three organizational building blocks. First, you have to understand your organizational DNA. Second, you have to set up the right reporting structure. And third, you have to design a budget that supports digital transformation.

Many digital leaders already know this. Our research and our digital CXO panels tell us there's a high correlation between organizational alignment and successful digital transformation. Whether you're a general manager or a top executive, the point is to move successfully from basic infrastructure tasks toward innovation.

How Ready Are You for Transformation?

Think about innovation along a spectrum, starting with an incremental process, which is sustaining innovation, to a transformational culture, which leads to breakthrough innovation.

When it comes to the transformational mind-set, there are four different categories of companies: market leaders, fast followers, cautious adopters, and laggards. Market leaders actively seek change, while fast followers react to market leaders. In a culture of cautious adopters, the politics are trickier than they are in market leader and fast follower organizations. Cautious adopters need to justify things. People are afraid to pull the trigger. Disruption is not impossible, but it is difficult. Market leaders and fast followers are folks who seek transformational change. If you're a cautious adopter, you're just dipping your toe in. You're probably not going to get there. Laggards, on the other hand, take a reactive approach. They don't see the benefits of change nor do they seek to proactively initiate projects. If you work for a laggard—well, good luck.

MARKET LEADERS

Market leaders represent just 5 percent of organizations. These folks want to proactively transform their business models. Their mind-set is, How do we transform? How do we change the world? They want to go to market first. They want to be the best. Their thinking is customer centric. They design things differently. They are relentlessly paranoid that the competition will catch up. They do not care what others think.

These market leaders truly want to differentiate their offerings. They want to be special. They are different. These are folks who want to co-innovate and co-create and build something new. Their companies are often run by founders—leaders who are unafraid. Think Microsoft, Oracle, Apple, Amazon, Facebook, and Uber.

Is that you? Does that describe your leadership team and larger organization? Is that where you want to go? Does that represent the spirit of your company? Market leaders are truly exceptional.

FAST FOLLOWERS

The next group is the fast followers. These organizations make up 15 percent of the marketplace. Fast followers sit at the intersection between reactive and transformational.

Fast followers are afraid to go first. But when they move, they move fast. They're ready to get the breakthrough innovations. That's what's important to them.

Fast followers ask questions such as, "What happens if our competitor goes first?" They're watching the competitors. They're watching the leaders. They're going to let them take the lead—but they are ready to move. They won't wait too long. What they want is to do things faster, better, cheaper, to learn from these first movers. Fast followers want to know what the first movers do and then ask, "How can we get there better? What mistakes were made?" Fast followers know they need to move. They're not going to spend a lot of time trying to develop those brand-new ideas. They just want to improve on those ideas, and they're not going to let anyone beat them there. These are important things within their digital DNA. It makes these fast followers very important.

CAUTIOUS ADOPTERS

The next group is cautious adopters. Like market leaders and fast followers, cautious adopters are proactive. And many are experts in the industry. The difference is, they like incremental innovation. So they study the issues.

In fact, they have whole sets of binders and studies. They've got reports. They hire consultants. They discuss issues for months—or maybe years. And when they move, they make small steps. They're afraid to make the big bets. They're afraid to cannibalize themselves. They're afraid to create new business models with no validation. They're worried about things like security and safety and risks. They're worried about the legal implications. They're wondering what happens to the rest of their market.

They lack leadership, so they can't seem to execute.

The good news? Half of companies around the world are like this. The bad news? Half the companies around the world are like this. That's what makes them cautious adopters. They are afraid, and that fear is what keeps them from being very successful.

LAGGARDS

The last group sits at the intersection between incremental innovation and being reactive. As you can guess, these are the laggards, who make up about 30 percent of the market. What these folks say is, "My business is doing great. I don't really need to change. There isn't that much margin. There isn't that much reason to actually invest in these new business models. In fact, we really don't need to disrupt our business. Customers aren't asking for this, so we don't need to deliver on it. All this crazy technology, and those folks out in Silicon Valley—we'll wait until all that stuff becomes commoditized, and we'll just pick it up for cheap. There's no need to go first, to make those mistakes." Laggards are really good at putting things off, and they're really good at adopting trends once they have become mainstream. That's what makes them laggards.

Cautious adopters and laggards represent many of the 52 percent of the *Fortune* 500 who have been merged, acquired, gone bankrupt, and fallen off the list.

Reporting Structures

The second organizational building block in creating a transformational culture is reporting structure. Reporting structure drives metrics. It drives conversations. Digital leaders who belong to executive management teams can play a strategic role in success. As a member of executive management, a digital leader can serve both as a utility and as a strategic adviser to the business. Unfortunately, in many cases some of these folks are not reporting at the right level. If you're reporting to a CFO, for example (and no offense to the CFOs out there), you're probably going to be relegated to a purely cost-centric, tactical position, because you're driving to those specific metrics.

It's important for everyone—not necessarily just the chief digital officer—to be a digital leader. But for that to happen, it's important that this transformational culture is infused into the reporting structure and that the executives who belong to the management team support that culture.

Budget

The third of these organizational building blocks is budget. At most corporations, basic activities—the core stuff, infrastructure—consumes anywhere from two-thirds to three-quarters of the technology budget—half of most of the operating budget or more—leaving very little for transformation. The goal, really, is to cut costs. In fact, most budgets follow the corporate hierarchy of needs. Think of Abraham Maslow's hierarchy of needs, where the idea is "Keep me safe, keep me healthy, keep me fed, keep me secure," all the way to personal identity and ego.

The same thing happens in the corporate world all the way up the brand. We have regulatory compliance at the very bottom level. Regulatory compliance is "Don't get me killed. Don't get me fired. And don't get me sued." Then operational efficiency, which is "For every dollar I spend, I'm going to save you three." Then we get to the next level, which is revenue growth. That's "For every dollar I invest, I'm going to make five. Well, maybe three." The next level is all about business model differentiation, and that's where transformation occurs. This is when we're trying to do something, create brand-new business models. And then, at the very highest level, is the ultimate goal of this digital business transformation: brand, where we keep our promises. And in that transformation, we are also changing what those promises are and how we deliver on them.

Unfortunately, most organizations' budgets are pyramid-like: heavy at the bottom and very light at the top. If you're going be successful in your digital transformation, you have to invert this budget pyramid so that you start thinking about the brand promise first and work your way down to the basics. This is the secret sauce that market leaders and fast followers have bought into—that inverted pyramid of needs.

Business Model Shifts

You're either going to disrupt or be disrupted in part of this transformation. As we all know, the pace of change has been intense. The incremental innovation that is out there is normal, but companies that follow that approach won't be able to keep up.

Consider the Sony Walkman. It was invented nearly thirty-five years ago. One could argue that this was Sony's big transformational innovation, the one thing that really put Sony on the map as an innovator. You could make the case that other products—perhaps TVs—did that as well. You could argue that PlayStation was an innovative part of Sony's identity. But other companies also had video game systems. You could say that Sony led in CD and DVD players. But they partnered with Philips, so Sony wasn't alone. You could talk about Sony's Trinitron technology, but that was before the Walkman.

Sony actually hasn't really innovated in the past thirty-five years. In fact, the company has been destroyed by others like Samsung because it hasn't had much transformative innovation. Sony's next innovation after the Walkman was the double cassette Walkman. It was cool. You could put two cassettes in the cassette case. You could play 180 minutes of music. I personally waited four or five years to get it. I couldn't even buy it in the United States—I had to go to Japan to pick one up.

But that shift from the Walkman to the double cassette Walkman was an incremental innovation. The transformational piece would have been an MP3 player.

Sony actually had three MP3 players. There were different divisions warring with each other within the company. The units were coming out at a time when Napster, LimeWire, and others allowed anyone to share music for free. You never had to pay for music again. These services, and their users, were flipping the bird to the music industry for, as they saw it, gouging customers for years by charging $20 for an album that really had only one to two good songs, and maybe a love ballad you could barely tolerate.

Let's be clear. Since Sony was also in the business of producing and selling music, there was no way it was going to cannibalize itself by introducing one of those three MP3 players into the market so that people could more effectively steal the company's music. So it sat on the technology.

At the same time, Apple decided to get into the music industry. And the company came through with a breakthrough innovation: the iPod. When Apple announced and launched the device, it was not the best-sounding music player. It didn't have the best battery life. It was actually predicted to fail because of these problems. It had a great interface, but its real success was the fact that it was a business model innovation. Apple got users to spend 99 times more for music that they could get for free. People were willing to go from free to 99 cents because they liked the iTunes store, they liked the ecosystem, and they liked the interface. Apple changed the music business.

Sony wanted to be Apple. Sony had all the digital IP and design—the same components Apple had. But Sony didn't want to cannibalize its existing music business with a new business model, so Apple eventually took that digital mantle away from Sony. Then Apple released another breakthrough innovation—the iPhone. The iPhone single-handedly destroyed twenty-seven business models.

We're talking about businesses that are never going to come back, businesses that were part of the 52 percent of organizations that have been eliminated, merged, acquired or fallen off the list of the *Fortune* 500. That's huge. It's everything. Where do you go to get your film developed? Not a one-hour photo shop. You don't do that anymore. Film's gone. Kodak's dead. What do you do when you want GPS? Do you get a Garmin or other navigation device? You don't need that. It's on your phone. What do you do to take a memo? Do you buy a little Casio recorder? No. What do you shoot movies with? A camcorder? You don't need that video camera anymore. You don't need a compass. You don't need a flashlight. You don't need an alarm clock. It's all on the iPhone.

Just look at the mobile business. If we go back to the year 2000, the companies that were going to be hot, the companies that were in charge of mobile, that were going to change the world, were BlackBerry, Microsoft, Nokia, Symbian. BlackBerry scoffed: Who wants a smartphone? Those things are ridiculous. But the fact was, this was the breakthrough innovation, the business model innovation that led the way.

The pace of change is fierce as these business models converge. Apple, seen as innovative, puts out one device a year. But that's not fast enough on the phone side. It's not fast enough on the tablet side. Samsung, which produces many of the components for Apple, puts out a new device every thirty to forty days. It might be a Galaxy S, it might be something else, but they put out a new phone every thirty-six days. They are putting out innovation at a faster rate, and some say maybe they're copying innovation at a faster rate. But the point is, Samsung wants to be Apple. And it could be.

This pace of change is massive in other industries as well. One of our clients, a clothing manufacturer in Sri Lanka, can deliver anything you see on a fashion runway in Milan or Paris into their customer's stores or into their contractor stores in seven to ten days.

Just being faster, just being better, just being cheaper is not enough. We're actually battling for something bigger in this transformation, which is why we're fighting for experiences and outcomes. We have to transform business models.

The important thing is to think about the metrics that really measure your business. Consider the airline industry. In the airline industry, the top metric is not safety. It's not on-time arrival. It's not customer satisfaction. For the airline industry, there's only one metric that counts: revenue per passenger mile. More money, more butts in seats. That's what matters.

In the airline industry, the hub-and-spoke model has been the predominant approach. You take lots of passengers. You create super-hubs. You get massive economies of scale. Then you fly everyone into a hub—whether it's Dallas or Chicago, whether it's LA or New York or DC or

Houston or Denver—for a stopover or connecting flight. You create these mega hubs, and you create a route system around that.

Incrementally innovating to get to those super-hubs is what happens if you decide that you need more butts in seats. Enter the Airbus A380. The Airbus A380 is a double-decker plane, similar to the double-decker McDonnell Douglas MD12 plane that was put out in the 1990s. The point is, you're putting more butts in seats. The Airbus A380 is an ultra-high-capacity airliner that can hold more than eight hundred passengers. That's a lot of passengers. This airliner is really designed for the traditional hub-and-spoke model. And that fact ultimately drives the revenue per passenger mile at the airline's convenience. That is the most important thing. It's also a bit more fuel efficient. That's the design point. So the A380 is set up to address the problems of revenue per passenger and fuel efficiency, but it uses the existing business model. That's incremental innovation.

But you can also address this problem in a transformational way. Enter the Boeing 787 Dreamliner. The Dreamliner is ultra light, ultra fuel efficient—and designed to do *point to point*. Wait, what's point to point? That means nonstop. Yes. It's basically an affront to the hub-and-spoke model. The way it is designed, because it is so efficient, allows you to create brand-new routes. So when the Boeing Dreamliner is up and flying, you're able to do crazy things like Osaka to San Jose. You could actually create a route from Indianapolis to Dubai, or Indianapolis to Belfast, if there's enough demand. And so it changes the hub-and-spoke model. It gets to what passengers really want to do, which is not have to make flight connections, not have to lose their luggage somewhere along the way. It also addresses revenue per passenger mile, but the Dreamliner reinvents the model at the customer's convenience.

The Dreamliner is transformational—so transformational that Airbus had to issue its own version, the A350 widebody.

This is what we want to do in our own industries: transform business models. And as we transform our business models, we create a transformational culture.

Let's look at companies, like Siemens, Philips, or GE, or health-care companies that sell big medical-imaging systems. They sell these devices at a million bucks each. You could buy one of these devices at a million bucks. You could then get a financing plan to pay for it over time. You could then get a maintenance plan to make sure the machine stays up and running. But when you're in the health-care industry, at least in America, or in a fee-for-service environment, the thing that matters the most is revenue per scan per hour. That's the metric that counts.

Remember, when you're thinking about transformation, you have to focus on the metrics that matter. So what do you want to see? How fast you can run these machines. You want to see how much bang for your buck you can get for them.

More important, these machines have to be up and running. So what does that mean? Well, when people look at that reality from a business model transformation perspective, they start to think, "Hey, if we could put sensors on these machines, and we could actually identify which parts fail first or fail more often than others, if we connect these machines into different networks and have those networks talk to one another, we could get to some very interesting business models."

And in fact, Siemens, GE, Varian Medical Systems, and a lot of other providers no longer care about just selling the machine. What their customers actually want—the outcome that matters—is up time. So instead of charging a million dollars for a machine and a service contract, these companies might say, "Look, let us guarantee you 85 percent up time over the next three years. We'll charge you

$3 million, and that will guarantee you 80 percent. If you give us $4 million, we'll give you 95 percent up time. That means if the machine ever goes down, we will drop off a brand-new machine if we have to, get it up and running, get you all set in two days max, so you have very, very little down time."

That's transformational. "And on top of that," the companies are saying, "we'll even manage the machines for you remotely, do proactive diagnosis. We're going to take care of all the parts. We're going to take care of failures. We can even provide benchmarking data." Why is it that a Johns Hopkins Hospital, a Mayo Clinic, a Cleveland Clinic, is more expensive than a community hospital out in Palo Alto? What's going on with these academic medical centers? How come they're making more per scan than the community hospital? Well, they can actually provide that benchmarking data. They actually know what parts are going to break down first. They know exactly how to build around it.

This is another example of digital transformation. Transformational culture involves thinking about how to change what customers want, and deliver to it. The transformational culture is, We're now going to shift to delivering on experiences and outcomes. The transformational culture is, We're going to use data to change the way we serve our customers. What you must build is an organization to do that.

Let's take Disney as another great example. For Siemens or GE or any other health-care provider, the goal was not to sell imaging systems. For Disney, the goal isn't to sell theme park tickets or another movie. Think about Disney's films. You started out watching a movie. You physically went to the theater. Then you might have picked up the VHS, and later you might get the DVD. When the latest technology released the same movie yet again, you might have gotten it on Blu-ray. You might even get it again by subscribing to Netflix. Think about this. You've bought, you've watched, you've acquired the same movie three to five times. What a great model for IP innovation. But there is more to the Disney model than just IP innovation. You might pick up an action figure or a book or another licensed product that features the movie's characters. You might actually go to a theme park. You might take a Disney vacation or go on a Disney cruise. There are even retirement communities in Bangalore, India, and in Celebration, Florida, that are Disney designed. And you're going to pay for the brand. You know you're going to pay more. You know the experience will be tightly scripted and controlled. You also know it's Disney, you know it's going to be family friendly, and you're OK with paying more. And this comes back to my point that Disney doesn't sell theme park tickets. Disney sells a promise. When you keep your brand promise, you keep your value. You can keep your margins. This is part of that culture of transformation, which is not only understanding the metrics that matter, but also understanding what brand promises you have to keep and designing and building everything from that brand promise.

This business model shift is already here. Customers know that we're no longer selling products or services—we're keeping brand promises. Product companies are giving away products for services revenues. They're giving them away against their margin. Products are being given away, and companies are making money on maintenance fees.

Service-based companies are trying to sell experiences at various price points, and on insurance plans, delivery, and installation. Experience-based businesses like Siemens, GE, and Disney are selling peace of mind by keeping brand promises. There is a natural hierarchy in this business model shift, and it's a big part of what we're talking about in business model transformation. First, you have to know yourself and understand your organizational DNA. Second, you have to figure out the difference between incremental innovation and transformational innovation. Are you ready? And then you have to think in terms of business model shifts that deliver on the brand promise. It's that brand promise that helps us get there, that helps us maintain our margins, that helps keep us disciplined in terms of how we innovate. And in terms of digital business model disruption, transformation is that first element that has to be achieved.

CHAPTER 3

DATA EXHAUST

HOW CONTEXTUAL RELATIONSHIPS DRIVE RELEVANCY AND ENGAGEMENT

Think of a person who walks into a bar in a new town and starts blabbing away without understanding the bar's environment. That's going to be a hit-or-miss approach to engaging in a new surrounding. The person doesn't even know if this is the neighborhood dive bar, a tourist bar, or a pickup bar.

Without looking at your surroundings, you can't know how people are connected to one another and what their angle is. Other folks in the bar can't tell if you're new to the town, if you're there on business, or if you're single. Everyone has to take the time to make observations and test assumptions along the way. The more time there is, the more interactions people can have, allowing them to understand the context and the relationships at play. This is basically "sense and respond." This is what creates the context behind authenticity—that sense and respond nature that we're constantly seeking to figure out how to refine the nuances and relevancy of experience.

Before the digital age, we had relevancy through our interactions, but not at scale. People's memories of a good shopkeeper or businessperson provided context. Good shopkeepers' reputations or brands were proven over time with each interaction. They remembered what you ordered, what you liked, what you disliked. The history of the relationship was built over time in formal and informal communications. Unfortunately, there was little recorded information in those transactions. But the frequency of interactions and the relationships built over time drove the strength of the relationships. Store owners trained their staff to remember their VIP customers' preferences and purchase histories. This delivery of context was what allowed the best merchants to differentiate themselves.

This level of personalization worked with a small set of customers and products with a limited number of inter-actions. Great shops were known for their personalized services and their ability to know what the customers wanted before they did. That ability to deliver based on context was critical to the authenticity of the merchant's brand and the authenticity of the relationship. In fact, that authenticity could not easily be copied by a new competi-tor. Those contextual relationships were a massive barrier to entry for competitors and a barrier to exit for customers.

But in the environment of digital business, things are different. Skill is required to bring back that shopkeeper level of intimacy between businesses and customers. Today, every "check-in," every "like," every purchase creates a digital footprint. And that digital imprint happens when no one is really looking. It can happen across any channel at any time, and it may not always be tracked or always provide a 360-degree view of interactions. This "data exhaust" is made up of everything we interact or engage with. These signals provide the context of our interactions.

The volume of data we capture is already beyond human comprehension. In 2013, 90 percent of the world's data had been created in the past two years, and 80 percent of that is what's called unstructured data, meaning clicks, comments, posts, pictures, chats, and so on. And while this digital exhaust often lives in different systems across the digital ether, the data is being aggregated.

Less than a decade ago, it was unfathomable that we could even capture all of those interactions, store that information, and glean insights. With today's computing power, we can do that with ease. The interaction data is different, though. We're no longer thinking in a world of CRUD—create, read, update, or delete—in those old, quaint, legacy transactional systems. But in a world where we can ask why something is liked or shared or published or responded to, we're changing not only how we interact with computers but also how we interact with one another. These systems' sense-and-respond nature is part of these systems of engagement. And in three to five years, we'll move on to systems of experience and mass personalization.

Interaction data recorded over time is at the heart of context. We're capturing as much data as we can to improve our understanding of context. What may seem like a tremendous amount of information is in fact only the beginning in this digital era. We've just begun putting sensors in everything from running shoes to jet engines. In addition, analog and digital experiences are converging and creating a very different world.

Pretty soon we will be drowning in all this data. We're going to hit the limits of a real-time world. We are already seeing that happen in these early years of social media. Every status update, every check-in, every post now elicits a groan. More and more, we are experiencing a real-time information overload. Real-time updates are creating dis-engagement because as soon as they are posted, the information is no longer relevant.

Think about the unfathomably bad experience we have with junk mail. If you're trying to stay authentic, you don't want communications that aren't relevant. It's noise when we already have tons of noise and very little signal. So how do we avoid drowning in this sea of information?

This is the conversation between real time and right time. What we long for is *right-time* relevancy. Delivery of the right information, at the right time, in the right mode, for the right situation, with the right priority level is what we're after. And how we get there is through context. Context is the key driver of right-time relevancy.

Which data should we capture? In their various relationships and roles, an individual can have multiple personas and should be treated as such. And each of those interactions basically takes us away from artificially forced-fit designations of business to business or business to consumer. The reality is that you might have different roles across the board. The main thing to think about roles is, Who are you? Who do you represent today? What's your identity? Roles are the part of context that we'll start with.

Then we have relationships. Are you a friend? Are you a new customer? Are you a prospect? Did you buy something in the past? What did you buy? How do you tie back to the company? Whom do you tie back to? Are you a loyal customer? Are you an angry customer? What's that relationship structure?

We have roles and relationships, and then there's time. When are you engaging? How often do you engage? And how long is that engagement? Time and frequency play a role because if you're passing through a train station at 5 p.m., versus passing through at 8 a.m., there might be something different.

We also have to think about physical location. Where are you located? Are you outside the building? Are you inside? Are you away from the shop completely?

The business process is also important. A customer might be in the middle of a process involving an order. How does that customer cut across different departments and functional fiefdoms if they buy a product online, return it in a store, and then use chat software for support? If you're asking a question about customer experience, if you're asking a question about order status, you're sitting in the middle of a fluid business process; things are going to be moved and put together like a choose-your-own-adventure book. The people inside organizations need to know where customers are in a process in order to address their concerns.

Sentiment plays a part, too. Is the customer happy? Is she sad? What is he feeling? How do we capture this? How do we know your mood at the moment?

Finally, we'd love to get to intent. Can we predict what you will do next based on your past behavior? What clues show you're willing to take the next action?

Roles and relationships, time and frequency, location, business process, sentiment, and intent—these are the context clues that provide us with the relevancy that moves us from real time to right time. A great example: by using your location data from cell phone towers, a local coffee shop can tell that you've passed by the shop during your morning commute ten times in a week, yet you've never stopped in. They might not know who you are: all they have is a signal that someone's phone number or SIM or ID number on a machine has passed by the store. So how do they tie that data to your social network?

Because if they were able to do that, the system and network could suggest that your friend buy you a cup of coffee at the shop you pass by but do not normally go into. Knowing a friend is there is a great way to entice you to stop on in and maybe change your habit. Maybe you don't want to reveal this level of personal information. But if you did, the coffee shop could also make you an offer based on previous purchases you've made through your phone and realize that, hey wait, you don't drink coffee. But maybe you'll come in for tea. The point is to get to a level of relevancy that can only be driven by context.

The problem is that we are drowning in all this data that we need to convert to information. It's coming from everywhere. There are sources ranging from nice little transactional systems, like a point-of-sale system or finance system or accounting system, to structured and semistructured sources like comments or blogs or posts or streams of tweets or likes. That is a lot of data.

We've got to bring that data to a point where we can get contextual. And to where we're using context, ultimately, to prove insight to make better decisions. But it starts with all this data, which we have to put into a channel of information that's both upstream and downstream. There's physical information, virtual information, machine information. We're trying to bring it all together. Once we've done that, then it becomes a question of getting to insight. We're using context to find insight or relevance around performance or deduction or inference or prediction.

What we want to do is achieve insight. How can we ask the right questions so that we can bring relevancy to the surface? What patterns are there that we've discovered about different groups of individuals or organizations? Ultimately, what we want to do is get to decisions, get to the next best action so we can present something tangible, so we can make a suggestion. Maybe we don't do anything. Maybe we use this right-time relevancy to continue to sense and respond.

But the point here is really that we want context to improve insight so we can make better decisions. All of this data—all of these digital exhaust demand signals—should help an organization figure out how to be more authentic to their brand. It's helping organizations understand how customers are reacting to suggested actions so that the organizations can stay authentic, not only to their brand but also to their base.

This leads us to a couple of things. First, in an authentic business, customers ultimately don't care what department you are in, but they expect the context to happen naturally. If the brand promise includes addressing customer service and improving customer experience or standing for something in particular, the quickest fail in authenticity comes on the call transfer. Every time a customer calls in about an issue and is told "Hey, let me transfer you to someone else," and then has to repeat all his information, it's a horrible experience. It's up there with having to tell every doctor in a hospital what your symptoms are every time they stop by to talk to you. We're trying to avoid the frustrations that come from an organization asking us the same questions over and over again. Organizations must be able to carry information so it's seamless.

Second, do it at scale. This is mass personalization. This isn't like the shopkeeper who knew you and kept that memory. This is the power of context as it carries across departments seamlessly and quietly in the background. The goal is not having to do all of this manually. The goal is for companies to predict future customer needs and wants because they actually have that information. It can be carried. It's contextual. It's relevant. And being able to do that at every interaction—that's what makes a business authentic. That's how it works in a digital world.

Zingerman's

A great case study about using context to help improve customer experience in an area of authentic business is the example of Zingerman's, a famous deli in Ann Arbor, Michigan.

In the summer of 2000, a newly engaged couple put in a large order with Zingerman's, which is known for awesome customer experience. They get context, they understand what people want, they take feedback, they have training sessions. Zingerman's had been a favorite spot for this couple. They wanted to have three hundred loaves of bread as a giveaway for their wedding—a thank-you gift that they wanted delivered.

This cargo was supposed to get to Zingerman's on the morning of the wedding, but it never arrived. And this is the wedding day. The bride's frantic, trying to figure out what happened. She calls the delivery company, which tells her, "Hey, we delivered them, they should be there." But the loaves of bread still haven't arrived two hours before the wedding's about to start. The couple calls again. The wedding coordinator calls. Still no loaves.

It seems like these customers aren't going to get these three hundred thank-you gifts. The guests are going to leave without any wedding favors. But on the other end of the phone during this process is a new hire named Jenna, who's part of the Zingerman's direct sales team. She's been listening to everything: the bride's upset, the wedding coordinator's mad, and so on. And Jenna's trying to figure out what's going on. She doesn't know where the driver is. And she doesn't know where these wedding favors are.

It's possible that none of this stuff will arrive. At the end of the day, she realizes that the big thing is, every order, every customer is important. The customer doesn't care about the fact that there may be a good reason why the driver didn't get there. The context of the situation here is that Zingerman's has to keep its brand promise. It delivers for its customers. The company ultimately must do this.

And so Jenna reaches out to the wedding coordinator and says, "Look, give me your three hundred guest names and addresses. We'll personally order a replacement loaf of bread for each guest and have them delivered to them at home." She's going to make sure that this happens. The bride's still furious, but she does send the guest list to Jenna. And the Zingerman's team decides, "Let's prepare three hundred gift baskets, let's do it up right, and deliver these replacement loaves. And let's send an apology note for what happened."

The interesting thing here is, Jenna knows that making this happen is part of the Zingerman's brand. She knows that customers don't care what department she's in. And she makes this decision as a new hire. This is a decision that's going to cost Zingerman's, too: first, for the three hundred loaves that didn't get delivered and then for another three hundred loaves that are now being mailed separately. This is a really expensive decision. This is a complete set of replacements, and they are being shipped all over the country.

And Jenna never checked with her manager. She never asked for permission. She knew that she had to do this. She never filed a purchase order. All she knows is, there's a really upset customer on the other end, and she represents a brand. And that brand promise is that they deliver their product when they say they will, and they deliver on making sure the customer is happy. Jenna represents the entire organization. She just did it.

One of the founding principles of Zingerman's when it was established by Paul Saginaw and Ari Weinzweig in 1982 was that employees should go to any length to deliver the Zingerman's experience—any length to keep the brand's promise. This is the shopkeeper example. This meant Jenna or her teammates could do anything within reason to leave the customer happier for having done business with Zingerman's. And the implication here is that in every interaction with the company, the company's reputation is on the line. Every team member's responsibility is to deliver on that brand promise. Even a very expensive decision made by a new hire is a small price to pay for that.

The urban legend of the missing loaves is that the van crashed and the driver died. But when we checked with Zingerman's, it turned out that the van had mechanical trouble and the driver was unable to contact Zingerman's headquarters. And the angry bride and groom story is now a cornerstone of ZingTrain, Zingerman's management training program, which corporations, nonprofits, and institutions throughout the world come to Ann Arbor to attend. And thanks to Jenna, Zingerman's not only re-earned the trust of the bride and groom but actually made three hundred new friends—three hundred new customers—by going to great lengths to keep that brand promise.

This is what happens in the analog world, where your customers don't care what department you're in. They just want you to anticipate and solve their problems, and because you know someone, you can get that job done. In the digital world, that is very hard to do. I don't know who the other person is. I don't know what they're doing. I don't know how customers view the experience they're having.

At the end of the day, every employee represents the organization, but how do you do make that count in a digital world? In an analog world, an angry bride and groom can call up your business, and you've got a way to keep them happy. In a world where everyone's chatting and the network never turns off, that angry call turns into an angry tweet. And it's not hard for that someone to destroy your brand representation. That's why in digital business, you really have to rely on context to understand who that individual is so that you can serve her better and so that every interaction a company has with a customer is done in a way that's authentic, that's true to the brand.

The good news is, you can do just what Zingerman's did: you—and every *Fortune* 500 company out there—can make that customer happy. The difference with a digital company is that it's not just good training programs and good recruiting. And it's not just good culture. We also need the ability to deliver on context. And this is where right-time relevancy plays a role. Customers operate in different channels. They don't care how you're getting your information. Context plays a role here. We've got to empower workers and employees so that information is being delivered at the right time.

More important, we've got to get better at response levels. And this is where context matters a lot. This is not just about real time. This is about right time. Customers may complain. They do complain. But hopefully, they also put some praise in there and reinforce the brand. So ultimately what we're trying to do with context is deliver.

This is mass personalization at scale, because what we're really delivering is right-time relevancy. Basically, we've made the shift from analog to transactional systems. This has led to a wave of automation-driven efficiencies in the past century.

Today we're in a world of engagement systems. And those engagement systems are moving toward experiential systems that are delivering mass contextual relevancy at scale, creating role-tailored communication styles, delivering bionic user experiences, and ultimately moving to right time and scale. We're shifting to mass personalization at scale, and those systems start with an outcomes-driven design point. We begin with the end goal in mind and work our way back. We're solving delivery of mass individual scale or customer segments of one. We're trying to craft personalized conversations. We're interfacing with human application programming interfaces (APIs) that enable people-to-people networks. We're talking about different technologies that can drive personal fulfillment.

Mass personalization at scale is here, and it's driven by context. We've gone from sense and respond and engagement, to agility and flexibility in experiences, to being intention driven. The challenge we're trying to solve in the engagement world is really about mass social scale. The challenge in experiential systems is contextual scale: trying to get to smaller and smaller segments of personalization. But ultimately, in mass personalization, we're trying to get to mass individual scale, which sounds like an oxymoron.

There are shifts in communication styles along the way. We've gone from being conversational to being very role tailored to ultimately having very personalized conversations, where a computerlike system—reminiscent of the hologram of the doctor in *Star Trek: The Next Generation*—is really having that kind of conversation with you. That's the early days of IBM Watson, when you think about where we are. And speed is a critical part of this. We're talking about moving from real time to right time to anticipatory in a space-time continuum. We're also talking about taking this context and going from corporate to personal networks, to segmented value chains in networks, and ultimately to people-to-people networks, which we'll talk about later.

We are now in a world where we've gone from business rules to predictive analysis to pattern-based thinking. New probabilistic algorithms are what's driving this, what's allowing us to serve up context at scale. And that's where mass personalization is heading. Let's take an in-depth look at Marriott, and how it is doing this at scale.

Marriott: Mass Personalization at Scale

Marriott has 325,000 associates worldwide and is organized around managed and franchised hotels. They're known as being one of the best companies to work for and are considered one of the world's most ethical companies. It's all part of the spirit to serve that came from J. W. Marriott Jr. and some other folks within the Marriott organization. The company has been focused on delivering that same level of experience to their Platinum Elite guests, those who spend something like seventy-five nights a year in a hotel. If you think about it, that's pretty brutal. Platinum Elites are on the road an awful lot.

At one point in my life, I was a management consultant for Ernst & Young. As a consultant, you spend half your life or more on the road, and you basically choose hotels based on price and location and on other things like phone call privileges, room service, location of the client—and so on. For one project I worked on, I spent nearly three months in the Boston area. Along the way, I got to know this general manager named Bill Munch, who managed the Marriott Copley Place in Boston and also the Cambridge Marriott. Bill ran an awesome customer-centric operation, before that term was even fashionable. Everyone from the bellhop to the housekeeper greeted you with a warm and sincere smile, no matter what they were doing. The customer service was excellent and beyond what you would expect from a chain hotel.

Let's be honest. Those hotels weren't in the best shape. They weren't super fashionable, like a W. These were just decent, business-class hotels.

Anyway, I'd stayed there for a long time, and that spring I really wanted to propose to my then-girlfriend and now-wife, Tina. So I pulled Bill aside one afternoon and told him, "Look, I'm going to be headed off to San Francisco in March. I want to propose to my girlfriend. Can you help me with an upgrade to an executive suite? Or just a larger room, something fun, kind of good for the weekend?"

So he got back to me and said, "Hey, don't worry about anything, we'll take care of you. We'll make sure everything's great."

There are a lot of different factors here. I really wanted to impress my girlfriend. I didn't want to give it away that I was going to propose. This was our first trip to

San Francisco together, and she was excited. And like any other guy proposing to his girlfriend, I was nervous as hell.

When I got to the registration desk at the San Francisco Marriott Marquis, the clerk looked up, as if he knew my name already. The guy's like, "Oh we've been expecting you, Mr. Wang. We've taken care of the upgrade. Bill Munch has called over here, so don't worry. We understand this is a special occasion, so just let us know whatever you need. We have your profile. You've got your extra sheets, you've got your extra pillows, and we've put you on a high floor as you requested in your profile. And by the way, we want to make sure that you come join us for dinner."

That was awesome. We decided to head upstairs. We wanted to take a look at what the room was like. So we got to the 34th floor with our bags and walked into the room, and wow. It was amazing. We were looking at 2,800 square feet. There was a huge vase of flowers for us. We saw a living room with a wraparound couch, an entertainment system. We saw this whole wonderful, large area and a dining room. The bedrooms were double the size you'd find in a normal suite. The bathrooms were the size of bedrooms. There was a 180-degree balcony. We were speechless and giddy. Bill Munch had done us good.

And later on that Saturday, I proposed, my girlfriend said yes—it was wonderful. We had an engagement party at the hotel for about a hundred folks.

Since then, I've been a loyal Marriott customer. Why? Because they delivered on my expectations, they understood context, and they have done it over and over again.

But it's not just that one incident. It's the fact that being a Platinum Elite guest actually means something. And that's really why it's important to try to understand what Marriott is doing. There's something magical about the way that the Marriott system works. Whether it's a franchise or a company-managed property, Marriott's associates start with the company's mission statement, and that mission statement is supported by context.

When I asked Rich Toohey, the head of Marriott Rewards, "What does that mission statement entail for Marriott?" he responded, "Attention to detail; openness to innovation; creatively serving guests; and pride in knowing that guests can count on the company's unique blend of quality, consistency, personalized service, and recognition at any Marriott property anywhere in the world." Sounds like every generic customer service mission, right?

But who works at Marriott is important. The hiring process is important. It's trying to find the right people.

It's looking for exemplary service—that's in the company's DNA. It's also helping to make sure that its associates actually have what they need to give customers their special hotel experience. For the top Marriott customers, Platinum Elite members, the service starts with this. But their experience involves more recognition in every service interaction. More benefits than other guests might receive. Ultimately, an elevated experience.

Marriott does this by using information and providing context, having a streamlined process, and of course, with training. At the information level, this is more than just customer preferences. It's capturing the profile online, or in an interaction with the clerk, or on the phone with the call center. In fact, all of these are at work all the time as each customer prefers different channels. Platinum Elite members are, first of all, likely to complete a profile, which helps provide context. But that profile is also being developed with every check-in. With every request, that interaction is captured. And so that information is there before the customer even arrives at the hotel.

And Marriott plans that. The staff knows at the beginning of every day who the Platinum Elite guests will be. Some of them even recognize those individuals and remember something about them and greet them by name when they come in. If you've stayed at the hotel before, they welcome you back.

At the process level, of course, Marriott is doing the right things. It has reports and procedures, and it can figure out room assignments and make sure people get the right room and the right benefits and the right welcome gifts when they walk in. And they can know that I'm allergic to feather pillows and prefer foam. That I want extra towels.

Part of how Marriott is able to provide this experience is through training. Staff members are trained to make sure that the Platinum Elite guests are given a unique kind of experience. So how does that work for the average Platinum Elite member? Well in fact, J.D. Power has given Marriott some really good rankings across the board—not just the flagship Marriott brand, but also a value brand like Springhill Suites. J.D. Power has listed them as number one for their upscale segment in 2012. Even the Marriott Ritz-Carlton brand has won top luxury category for the third or fourth year in a row. And one of the ways they do this is they actually create different types of experience, and that happens because of context.

The Marriott experience is really about empowering an entire organization. It's basically trying to do Zingerman's approach at scale. Imagine doing that even more at scale in a digital world. This would be beyond reservation teams. This is every single travel site that's out there, plugging into the Marriott experience. Marriott is trying to carry their authentic brand to people who are not even customers.

To do that, housekeeping, reservation, food service—every department—has to deliver the same high level of customer experience. And they have to have a level of context to understand how to do this in the same way that Jenna, the Zingerman's employee, was able to do.

Marriott's Platinum Elite status is basically a marketing program that represents the business. It's about Marriott's "way," their spirit to serve. And the entire organization knows that Platinum is the code for doing whatever it takes within a wide set of boundaries—taking that context and personalizing it. Because when a person decides to spend money with Marriott, every staff member, whoever they are—whatever the interaction or engagement—must be there to serve. They should be there to provide that personalized experience. And context is how they get there.

So where does that take us? We need to think about ways to engage with context. And this engagement map, this journey map in the digital world is actually what's being successfully delivered in a digital world. This journey map is what helps a business be authentic. And what we want to do is engage with context for what is termed right-time relevancy.

There are nine things to get you there, what I call the "nine Cs."

The first three Cs encompass what we call people-centric values. These are things like delivery and communication styles and right-time contextual drivers. These values involve trying to understand what our customers seek. We're trying to understand the culture, the community, the credibility. We're trying to listen in. This is the sense piece in sense and respond. The first three Cs of developing context with customers include:

- **Culture.** What are the norms? What are the communication preferences? What are the global outlooks? What preferences and styles does the customer bring at the moment of engagement? How can we best sense those kinds of cultural cues?

- **Community.** This is about segmenting customers based on internal and external points of view, right? External communities could be customers, partners,

DISRUPTING DIGITAL BUSINESS

suppliers, or influencers. Internal communities could include employees, the board of directors, contract workers. But ultimately these are different groups of people. These could also be arranged by family. These could also be arranged by other segmentation models. And so community is really the segmentation model that's here.

- **Credibility.** How do we represent trust? Where do influence and reputation and records and authority and appearance come into place? Because effective communications do require credibility, which we'll talk about.

The second set of Cs is around delivery and communication styles. Here, what we're trying to figure out is, What have we learned that determines how we will communicate? What channels do we go into? What content do we deliver? How often in terms of cadence do we get in? We know this based on our assessment of the people-centric values. This is the infrastructure that allows us to respond. The three communication styles are:

- **Channel.** What do we engage with? Today's channels are anything from in-person interactions to

Data Exhaust

kiosks to the web to social media to mobile phones.
The question is, How do we map these channels
to what customers expect? Ultimately, customers
don't care what channels you're in. They only care
about the channels *they* are in. This goes back to the
analog example where customers didn't care what
department you were in. Basically, they're engaging
with you, and that's all that matters.

- **Content.** So now that they're in front of you,
  what are you delivering to help them to engage
  successfully? Content is the information, what we're
  delivering. It could be internal, user generated,
  repurposed, or paid news analysis. Ultimately, we're
  delivering content. So what are the results and
  byproducts of these interactions with customers?
  And how can they be used not just once, but
  repeatedly?

- **Cadence.** This describes when or how often you
  plan to engage. Cadence can be ad hoc. It can be
  scheduled or designed as part of an experience, or it
  can be continuous. For example, designed cadence
  occurs when you buy a new electronic or mobile
  device or product, and on day one, the provider

63

sends you a new tip: "Come register with us." On day two, the provider might say, "Hey, have you tried this feature yet?" On day three, the provider asks, "Do you want to share something that you know with a friend?" Cadence is the frequency and manner in which you engage.

So we've got the people-centric values—the culture, community, and credibility. And we have the delivery and communication styles, which are channel, content, and cadence. Now you have the tools to actually deliver what you're going to do next. This is where the right-time contextual drivers—context, catalyst, and currency—come in. These are the elements that will set you up to create meaningful interactions, meaningful engagement. It's where we get the call to action.

- **Context.** This is the relevancy. It's where we're drawing on the network through relationships and roles. It's where we're going back to time, location, and business process. But ultimately, context is built on the fact that we sense the people-centric values. We know what channels and context and cadence to deliver to. And so context is where we ask, What is the appropriate path?

- **Catalyst.** Here's where we have the call to action. The catalyst is what inspires action and response. Catalysts egg you on to do something: whether to show up, whether to respond, whether to participate in a loyalty program, whether to look at an advertisement. But catalysts have to appeal to the customer's self-interest, values, and styles. The basic question here is, How do we improve engagement with context? This is how we make things relevant. And so the catalyst is that offer that gets you to respond, hopefully in a positive way.

- **Currency.** Currency is the actual influence mechanism. How will we exchange value and influence behavior? Monetary incentives include cash, bonuses, rewards, and rebates. Nonmonetary currencies could be knowledge, virtual goods, recognition, access, or influence. Right? How do customers get rewarded for engagement? We did some studies with a client where we had fifty new banking associates that came in with salaries of $250,000. They were given the option to take a $50,000 bonus, spend a day with the CEO, have a mentor that they'd meet with once a month, work on a special project, or do a volunteer activity once a month that they could take the day off for. Ultimately, only two took the money. These other factors, in terms of access and influence, were much more important to the other forty-eight employees than just cash. So you can actually see where monetary and nonmonetary incentives play a role.

No matter how we get there and how we engage, ultimately, context plays a huge role in getting to right-time relevancy. The more we can rely on context, the more we can actually deliver on an authentic business.

CHAPTER 4

BEING FOX NEWS

WHY TRUST AND TRANSPARENCY ENABLE AUTHENTICITY

Trust drives influence, engagement, and relationships. Gone are the command-and-control relationships of the past. People and organizations must earn trust through their actions across their relationships. Trust can be expanded to gain influence, create engagement, and foster relationships. Trust can also be lost if you lack credibility, or if you show dishonesty or other bad behaviors.

Perhaps the most crucial characteristic of a digital business is how easy it is to initiate and break a relationship. The speed at which we establish connection is a double-edged sword, because it's just as easy to switch off when trust and transparency are broken. That's why in the case of digital business, every interaction is predicated on establishing and reestablishing trust. Every connection point is vulnerable. Every node only connects when there is some level of trust. Some nodes have a lower tolerance, others higher. Just as those nodes are seeking trust on the demand side, the sell side is pushing for trust just as much. If companies could buy the trust, they would. However, you can't just buy influence and engagement in the digital world.

In the digital world, you have to earn trust, and transparency is there to validate that trust. The good news? Digital functionality brings greater transparency than ever before to every transaction. This helps us validate trust with every signal, every interaction. Transparency helps us build trust based on our previous actions, intentions, and other sources of insight. Transparency helps us have confidence that our past can allow us to establish trust with others and thereby secure our future.

This is why trust and transparency are often interrelated. This is why we're putting them together here. Trust relies on verification and opens the door to relationships. Transparency is that verification that requires no trust. A trusted network is a net that can catch a falling elephant, and a network with broken trust is that same network with an elephant-sized hole in the middle, and a dead elephant.

Whom we choose to pass information onto—whether we choose to engage with a person or, somehow, a machine—how we evangelize about a product or service or when we endorse a firm we've done business with all depend on this trust and transparency relationship in business.

In digital business, we have to remember that there are three key entities in the trust and transparency equation. First, there's the trusting entity. Second, there's the trusted entity. And third, there are all these outside influences. The trusting entity is the individual group, machine, or ecosystem that's requesting to engage. They are open. They are trying to connect. These are people and their networks that want to make the connection. They could be buyers. The trusted entity is the other half, the part that the trusting entity is asking to connect with. The trusted entity is selected for value exchange and is the connection point requested, receiving a request to engage. That's when we have this pull, push, pull, push, tug here between people trying to figure out, Do I engage? Do I not engage? Do I engage? Do I not engage? In this decision, the outside influencers are connected to the network and can influence the levels of the trust based on what the trusting entity and the trusted entity believe.

In a corporate world, in corporate brands, in a digital world, trust is the new currency. Radical transparency is inevitable, and authenticity is earned—not faked. Trust and transparency drive this key part of digital business.

So the three things to remember are: trust is the new currency. Radical transparency is inevitable. Authenticity is earned, not faked.

Trust

So what does trust mean in a digital world? There are seven elements of trust that are important in this environment:

- **Durability.** How long have you been developing a history based on interactions over time and collected among data points? Put another way, How long has your firm been trusted, and by what standard? Seven straight years in a row of earning J.D. Power and Associates awards is an old-fashioned example. In the digital world, we're talking about how often you've been praised on Yelp for your services, if you're a restaurant, or if you've received kudos from highly rated experts or influencers about your product over time from relevant sources. This durability is important. Durability is the foundation of trust.

- **Consistency.** Consistency measures not just how long a business can maintain trust but under what circumstances. Can you deliver the same level of quality or better with each interaction for that service level? Are you consistently keeping your promises? That's an important part of establishing trust.

- **Competency.** Competency is the demonstration of achievement. If durability and consistency are about not violating expectations, competency is about living up to them. Competency is about how well a company succeeds, not simply how well it keeps from messing up. In a world where we no longer merely sell products or services but have moved to outcomes and experiences, can you consistently deliver on that brand promise, and for how long? And how do you get there? As you can see, durability, consistency, and competency are very closely related.

- **Timeliness.** Timeliness enables open and honest communication. You've got to be timely in terms of your response. You've got to be timely in terms of your communications. You've got to be timely in terms of delivering information quickly and as openly as possible with each other. Timeliness is an important factor in establishing trust, because if you're withholding information, or if it seems like you're late on something, people are not going to trust you.

- **Meritocracy.** Meritocracy is especially important in the digital world. It involves the need to distribute fair rewards for actions. In other words, you have a value system where if you treat people right, they will participate and interact, and they will be rewarded for that in certain ways. But this is really about customer participation. Think about it. Companies should not expect customer participation without rewards. But the reward can't just be tied to who shouts the loudest. A system based on meritocracy means that rewards are distributed according to who does the most good for the company's entire network. Who does the most good for the other trusted entity? That's not just a simple set of circumstances. This idea of meritocracy helps people understand that there's an implicit bargain in play for simply engaging or for certain types of actions.

- **Accountability.** Accountability means that you will do what you say you'll do. Small deviations from this promise actually nibble away at your trust.

They widen the brand promise that you are out to deliver. Accountability is important. Stakeholders need to know who's in charge, and for what actions. Accountability sets expectations as to what will be delivered and what will happen if expectations are not met. You are judged by your actions and your inactions here.

- **Respect.** Companies are by definition designed to create a level of respect and trust. You have to treat companies like people. For people, the trust that's required by mutual respect is the corporate brand. That brand must respond like an individual. And there are different ways to get there. But however it happens, companies need to build a sense of respect between parties and see customers as people, even lots of people, rather than open wallets. Companies have to take the view that there needs to be respect in each customer relationship and be out to prove that. Respect has a lot do to with what's going on in the trust side.

These seven elements are what drive the trust equation. As I mentioned earlier, trust and transparency go hand in hand. If trust is a new currency, radical transparency is inevitable. In fact, we're entering a world of radical transparency. In this digital world, there's no hiding the truth. It's everywhere. It's almost as if every day is a day on *The Truman Show*. Our actions and interactions are consistently being tracked. There is a level of openness in digital that is crazy. The ability to build interaction histories becomes the foundation of this new transparency.

It's not just the history of interaction that makes transparency inevitable, it's the speed. The time it takes information to travel is measured in milliseconds. Transparency happens instantly. It's the foundation of open and honest communication. Think about this: trust is about taking a person at his word, and it's required when there's a lack of transparency.

But when you have both transparency and trust, digital networks gain optimal efficiency, because everything that is carried along the network can be measured. And transparency is measured—this is the data aspect. All this data and all this information is the foundation of digital business, and this data is providing us this transparency to really act on what's next. But transparency is a hard thing to sell inside the companies we work with.

Most companies associate transparency with either endangering intellectual property or simply being less invincible or sharing information that could be conceived as a competitive advantage. But that's not what we're talking about. We're talking about transparency as the acknowledgment that we're living in a digital world, that all that history is in front of us, behind us, around us. And how we share that interaction history, how we share that transparency with one another is what's important, what makes these digital business networks effective. In some cases, we don't even have a choice about how that information will be distributed, because we've left a trail. It's been captured by others during their screening process. There is no digital disposal mechanism for this digital exhaust. Attempting to hide, conceal, or equivocate your actions—well, that becomes a very expensive denial of reality that adds friction to the process and makes digital business very hard to succeed at.

Because we are living in an era of radical transparency, the question is, How do we improve that transaction transparency? Where does radical transparency exist? How does radical transparency take hold in digital business? And what does it mean? Here are some factors to consider:

- **Engagement points.** Every channel, every connection is now open. People understand these connections. They can be measured, whether it's a face-to-face interaction (which is less measurable), an SMS text or other mobile connection, or a sensor or other analogical system. Every engagement point is now an area for radical transparency. Actions are being tracked. What was done? Who bought something? Who connected? Was the product delivered? Was it returned? Was it a good process? Every action is part of this.

- **Content.** Content is experiencing radical transparency in digital. This can be anything from the sharing of a comment that you thought was hidden to a product or a price. Content can be created, read, updated, shared, and trashed. But in the case of transparency, as we're talking about here, content reflects both what you want to say and what you want people to think. It could be earned, owned, or paid in terms of what has been delivered around you.

- **Chronology.** "When" becomes very important. What was the sequence of events? What result did they lead to?

- **Location.** The "where" is also critical in developing transparency. Where did the action happen? Where was something already in motion? At what node does this action occur? Where in that process did it occur?

- **Product.** In cultivating transparency, people want to know what was exchanged. Was it monetary? Non-monetary? What currency was the product traded in during this interaction?

- **Truthfulness.** Was the interaction truthful? How do you compare this truthfulness, or veracity, over time?

These areas are all driving the fact that trust and transparency improve authenticity. And authenticity is key.

Fox News

In a digital world, organizations are competing to deliver on brand promises. Those promises are held by trust and transparency. This means that the organization is always the product. The collection of individuals and nodes that form networks in a digital business has to be trusted and show transparency. Because authenticity is earned and cannot be faked in this environment, every node has to be trusted. When they're not, the brand is in jeopardy of losing its authenticity. Maintaining that authenticity is an important part of disrupting digital business models.

Many organizations, though, are stuck in the mind-set of an earlier era. They don't let their employees develop distinct credible public brands. In fact, most organizations do not know how to balance an individual's personal brand with the corporate brand. Yet, one organization that has allowed this employee independence and brand identity is Fox News.

Fox News is known for a lot of things: conservative politics, questionably accurate slogans, the watchful stewardship of Roger Ailes and Rupert Murdoch. But it has also developed the strongest brand of any news network out there. It's conservative, aggressive, and opinionated. And it puts its trust and transparency on the line every day. It's a network of personal brands that builds authenticity. In a June 2014 poll from the Brookings Institution, Fox News was named the most trusted news source in America. When people were asked to name the television news sources they trusted the most to provide accurate information on politics and current events, 25 percent answered Fox News. MSNBC came in dead last. And this was a wide sample—conservative, moderate, and liberal.

How does this happen? Fox's brand may be the conservative news network—in other words, not what you might call fair and balanced—but it's also the home of a number of folks that people trust, whether it's Sean Hannity or Greta Van Susteren or Mike Huckabee or Bill O'Reilly. These on-air talents are each given ample room to promote their own personal brand and build that trust and transparency. What's more, they occupy different facets of Fox News's brand personality: Sean Hannity, blue collar, jockish; Mike Huckabee, folksy, corn-fed; Megyn Kelly, hard charging, direct; Greta Van Susteren, a former friend of Secretary of State Hillary Clinton, someone who can talk to the other side.

And then there's Bill O'Reilly, who's the most combative of the bunch but who takes great pride in avoiding easy characterization. He will be the first to tell his critics that he's the loudest mouth on Fox News, but he's also against the death penalty and supports gun control and environmental regulation. O'Reilly's personal brand, arguably the most successful of all those on Fox News, seems to be, "I'm not quite as Fox News as you think I am." And what's interesting about this is that it builds authenticity. That builds trust and transparency in terms of where he's coming from. Fox News actually gives O'Reilly, like the other personalities it employs, plenty of time to advance his personal brand. In any broadcast, there are at least five mentions of www.billoreilly.com. O'Reilly puts out appeals to over twenty-five charities he supports, including the Wounded Warrior Project, Fisher House Foundation, Doctors Without Borders, Tuesday's Children, New York City's Coalition for the Homeless, and the Haitian Health Foundation, and he openly promotes his books on-air.

Would Brian Williams or Scott Pelley or any one of the major anchors on other channels get that type of self-promotional latitude? Even on CNN? Picture any of these news anchors without their networks. Do they have a personal brand at all? Diane Sawyer, maybe, from years of doing in-depth interviews, first at CBS. Brian Williams barely exists in the public mind. In fact, NBC has had to offer a little help in terms of his branding with greater pro-motional spots throughout its daily programming. And Scott Pelley? Wait, who's that?

People on news channels are also trying to fill hours and hours of airtime. They have to become comfortable with personal opinion and personal brands, rather than follow-ing the protocols put in place by the old-line networks. MSNBC has tried to follow in Fox's personality-driven footsteps with maybe a little success, even though it came in last in the Brookings poll in terms of news (it is seen more as entertainment than as news). And CNN keeps trying.

Fox News has been criticized for paying only lip service to objectivity, and it is therefore seen as giving its talent total freedom to voice opinion and be self-promotional. But that's not true. Fox has also been disciplined and removed talent for a personal brand and self-interest that seemed too far afield from the network's brand. Look what happened to Glenn Beck when he passed beyond the trust and transparency spectrum. The lesson of Fox News within this trust and transparency framework is pretty clear. Employees have their own networks. They develop their own trust and transparency. The collection of those networks creates these personal brands around authenticity. These authentic brands actually form the larger basis of what's going on with trust and transparency for an organization. And an organization can benefit from these personal brands, these nodes of their employees' personal brands, where they strike a good balance between how these two brands benefit each other. And this is very important. In fact, what we're talking about as trust and transparency comes at every node.

Trust and transparency are built over time. They're actually what are allowing us to build authentic brands in a digital world. And they come from not only people. Trust and transparency come from the fact that the nodes are trusted. There's an authenticity, there's a promise behind those brands that's being delivered. And there's an important part of digital business in one of these pillars because trust and transparency drive the authenticity that's required to disrupt digital and drive success.

Bitcoin

Bitcoin is a digital currency created by an anonymous founder, or founders, who use the name Satoshi Nakamoto. Nakamoto posted the original design to an obscure cryptography mailing list on January 3, 2009. The idea: digital money could enable instant payments to anyone anywhere in the world in an anonymous and secure manner. In a 2011 profile of the programmer in the *New Yorker,* writer Joshua Davis called Bitcoin "all bit and no coin," which is a really good point, given that this was a complete digital currency. Since the dawn of the internet, many people have attempted to create a digital equivalent of cash, and a lot of them have failed. That's because they relied on a central authority within an existing global financial system to support a disruptive alternative. That's just not going to happen. These central authorities would play a role in tracking the creation and expenditure of the currency, which would defeat the purpose. People didn't want to be tracked. This is the disruptive nature of a cash system that's direct, which in a P2P world is very different from a centralized currency system. All monetary systems depend on a degree of trust, and traditional currency is about trust in the currency itself and in the issuing body. At a time when people don't trust their governments' monetary policies and how they're printing more money than the countries are worth and inflating currencies and so on, this is a great problem.

Digital currency depends on that kind of trust, plus something else: trust in the system and all its participants. It has to function differently. Bitcoin doesn't rely on a central authority that manages transactions and issues currency. In fact, the network manages itself, which lends trust and transparency. Money is mined through this interesting algorithm with an absolute limit of 21 million coins. It can't inflate the coins. This cryptocurrency can't be inflated, manipulated, or impacted by political pressures, like if we need to raise money for a war or we have to drop interest rates. So, as with all currency and stored value mechanisms, the value depends on the currency holder's belief that a bitcoin is worth something. So trust is paramount.

This is a great example of trust and transparency. The reason previous systems have failed is that people were trying to figure out how many times a unit of currency was used and who used it. Bitcoin solved this problem by having a third party manage a ledger of all these transactions and then releasing the ledger to the public in a peer-to-peer fashion. It's one of the things that makes Bitcoin unique—building that trust.

How did Bitcoin establish trust in the currency? By using the seven trust factors we talked about earlier. First, Bitcoin's encryption is *durable*. It's been shown and proven. It's been going since April 2010. People see how these things are mined. It's been going on long enough. There have been trading networks.

Second, there's *consistency*. Exchanges ensured a safe and secure way to convert bitcoins into other currencies. And the value of bitcoins definitely is not being inflated or manipulated.

Competency—well, people are actually accepting bitcoins as currency. In June 2014, the State of California accepted Bitcoin as a payment mechanism. And this has added to the level of trust. Also, it's very hard to steal a bitcoin.

The public ledger chain shows a predictable money supply that you can't hyperinflate. This *timeliness* of information that shows how this money rate occurs keeps mischief from happening.

Bitcoin also has a *meritocracy* system, where the mining of cryptographic puzzles unlocks fifteen new bitcoins to those who solve them. So exchange for value immediately occurs when you mine a bitcoin by using computing processing.

As for *accountability*, only 21 million bitcoins will be produced. Despite anonymity, bitcoins are spent and stored in a public ledger chain that's decentralized and transparent to everyone.

And finally, because of the anonymity of bitcoin, every user or holder of value is theoretically treated the same. That's *mutual respect*. There's no discrimination in the use of a bitcoin. In fact, your anonymity and privacy are being respected.

Bitcoin has succeeded because of these seven trust factors. They are what drove the initial adoption of Bitcoin.

But that trust has started to erode. Bitcoin, like other cryptocurrencies (Canada's cryptocurrency, MintChip, is an example), is losing some level of trust because the original design produced 21 billion units of currency. Because people knew it was finite, they started hoarding. And hoarding transformed what was a digital asset from a currency to a stored speculative value. Bitcoins were now bet on like stocks, and it's hard to control when there's no regulation to other forms of cash. So trust is eroding over time.

This is a great example of lessons learned on trust and transparency, especially for corporations. Those seven trust factors are critically important. And we also see that over time, you could lose all that trust if you don't promote those factors. When you don't focus on durability, consistency, competency, timeliness, meritocracy, accountability and mutual respect, trust and transparency are lost.

CHAPTER 5

A GLIMPSE INTO THE FUTURE

BUILDING AN INTENTION-DRIVEN MIND-SET

Digital businesses start with an intention-driven mind-set. We're talking about systems that can predict the next best action. These systems are more than smart. They learn on their own. They sense and respond and mimic sentience. They mine a wide variety of data sources. They take bits of data or streams of signals and align them to business processes like a marketing campaign or financial close or an order or even a workflow for HR. They're almost human. They know how to connect, and that's what makes them interesting.

These smart systems surface patterns, and those patterns then lead to insight. So the systems are basically taking all this data, translating the information, bringing up insight, and ultimately making decisions. Organizations that develop these systems may ask themselves, "Why are blue sweaters selling better in Ann Arbor, Michigan, and red sweaters selling better in Birmingham, Alabama?

Could it be because of college sports teams in those areas? Why do sweaters sell better in college towns in September than in December? Could it be the start of the school year? Or is it the availability of financial aid?" Surfacing patterns and answering questions are a key part of this process in intention-driven systems.

Armed with these insights, digital businesses work toward precision decisions. We know now not to order as many blue sweaters in Alabama. We also know to stock more sweaters in August and September, and fewer in December. And while we feel very comfortable with the autonomy of human judgment today, over time, digital businesses will automate many of these human-made decisions, to the point where human interaction is no longer required. In fact, we'll expect the system to make the suggestions and keep going until we tell it otherwise, or when it suggests that a pattern has changed.

These patterns come from various data points. They are the foundation of digital business. And they provide the background for intention-driven systems. As each pattern for moving from data points to decisions is analyzed, these systems will learn from each interaction and improve their precision. Decisions are crunched. Models are modified. And we go back to the beginning. We take the data and crunch it. We put it into information that ties back to business processes.

These business processes surface insights that tell us how to take action and make the next best decision. This is the nature of an intention-driven design point, and there are four important areas that drive it: self-awareness, sentient systems, predictive models, and augmented humanity—that is, self-learning and cognitive capability.

Intention-Driven Design

Intention-driven design starts with self-aware sentience. As organizations build digital models in their physical world, everything from sight, sound, smell, taste, humidity, and touch are coming through sensors and analytical ecosystems. Digital equivalents of analog systems and even humanity are being delivered.

Cameras play a role today in our visual senses. We have listening devices that are more than audio—they can detect vibration. Other instruments from the speedometer to the durometer, the accelerometer inside your phone, take down acceleration and position. Even climate is being integrated into digital business systems to determine if humidity, temperature, or weather could impact a decision. These sensing networks and their related sensor and analytic ecosystems are the front lines for intention-driven design. And these networks that were once isolated are now set up in a connected world of ecosystems that take these data points and broker them to both the consumer and enterprise worlds. Smart machines and wearables are providing new types of sensors that add to the mix of data that's creating insights. Constellation Research estimates that at least 200 million smart wearables will ship by 2018. These are bracelets. These are fabrics. These are watches. These are eyewear. These are any sensor-embedded devices worn by a human. They can even be connected to humans through human APIs and neural networks. Data from automobiles and medical devices and household appliances, as well as from power generators and building systems, are providing opportunities to improve operational efficiencies, create new business models, and identify new usage patterns.

These systems will not only communicate with one another, but also interface with people, overtly and covertly. The Internet of Things moves from an abstract concept to a living and breathing machine-to-machine meshed network interfaced with humanity. These could be human

APIs. These could be new ways to connect through sensor neural networks.

By 2020, the global market for a few billion cell phone SIMs will swell to 100 billion MIMs—machine ID modules. Technologies will include a 100-gigabit optical network—and that's robotics and manufacturing, building management systems, MIMs, geolocation drones, self-driving cars, smart grids, and software-defined networks. There's a quantum leap in the quantity and quality of information coursing through these digital businesses.

In fact, digital business disruption is happening right in front of us, and data is the foundation of these digital businesses. As a result, manufacturers are remodeling their factories' shop floors. They're trying to figure out how to mimic and how to model and how to forecast what could happen. Retailers are remodeling the shopping experience to see where and why customers engage. Logistics companies are tracking routes and warehouse movements. In the consumer world, home automation and wearables are just the beginning of the sensored data connected to power these new models. Wearables such as Fitbit, Nike, Jawbone, Apple Watch, and Samsung are just the beginning. Nest and Apple iHome modules are just a glimpse of what's next. The car is also one of the next battlegrounds as we're looking at sentience in machines. This is also happening in advanced fiber technology and electronics. There's convergence to create smart textiles—where material science meets the digital age. E-textiles can sense and respond to a range of environmental stimuli. We're talking everything from monitoring capabilities like internal signals such as heart rate, perspiration, and skin pH to external elements such as CO_2, temperature, humidity, and sunlight. The textiles can then respond through an alert or even a change in color or pattern.

Surfaces such as smart glass also play a role in how information will be captured, presented, shared, and interacted with. In fact, advances in material sciences are playing a critical role in enabling intention. So when we combine these data and signals, we enable improved context.

How do we take all this data and bring out intent? It requires significant orchestration. As these sensor and analytical ecosystems mature, digital or electronic or interface message processors (IMPs) emerge to bring embedded hardware and software platforms together, to connect networks of devices and wearables to work with one another. And they're working in a similar way to how interface message processors worked in the early days of the internet to connect computers.

Now we're connecting every end point. Almost every individual is an IP address. Devices allow manufacturers and developers and networks and machines and people to manage and scale with one another and to create networks that support intent. These are where we're getting our data, and this is why we're seeing self-aware sentience. This self-aware sentience is creating sense-and-response capabilities.

Probabilistic Models

The second part of being intention driven is following predictive or probabilistic, not deterministic, models.

I know, that sounds like a mouthful, but what's been happening is that organizations have trained themselves to identify their best business processes, to standardize them in order to improve quality or meet regulatory requirements. The results have moved organizations forward. When they were first introduced, these deterministic rules were great. They led to guided selling techniques, service checklists, marketing funnels, and loyalty journey maps. Unfortunately, these were the best practices of the 1980s, carried over into the 1990s, codified in the 2000s, and now we're stuck with these fixed processes. That's what we call deterministic. These approaches worked brilliantly for companies then, but today we are saddled with a set of fixed rules that no longer apply to how an organization works or responds. Especially in the digital world.

Now we're moving away from deterministic areas toward probabilistic ones. And what's happening here is really a war for algorithms. This is the death of deterministic models. Those fixed rules worked for systems of transaction, which were nice, neat little systems, and they worked for some systems of engagement. But at the digital scale, there is no right pathway. There is no correct journey map. In a world of mass personalization at scale, there's only the probability that what lies ahead might be the best path. At times it's going to seem undefined.

Given the current conditions, the probabilistic model is probably going to be the right way to go. Digital brings all these probable outcomes together and surfaces them based on what's most likely to happen. So probabilistic models have grown in importance. These are coming from machines learning algorithms, artificial intelligence. They're sensing. They're predicting. They're inferring. And in some ways, they're even thinking. Systems are gleaning insights from past behaviors on current conditions and translating them into predictions of future models.

What these systems are trying to figure out is, will something happen? Is it going to happen again? Why does it happen? The predictions aren't 100 percent accurate, but we're trying to make those decisions precise. We want to accurately guess what the customer may want to do next or what a system needs to do next.

So it's no longer black and white. Everything is fifty shades of digital gray (i.e., #d3d3d3 for the geeks in the house). Why? Well, armed with the perfect context, probabilistic models can generate precision decisions. To achieve mass personalization at scale, these models have to suggest the best set of decisions at a point in time. That's the key here—a point in time. The logical conclusion is, then, that the next battleground in digital business will be math—yes, math. The best algorithm's going to win.

These algorithms are basically small programs and sets of instructions. In a digital world, we need the ability to quickly assemble small units or composable sets of code and algorithms. It's where the battle lines begin. How these composable bits of code work with algorithms is the secret sauce inside organizations. That's the core intellectual property. These exist. They're happening. We already see early versions of them in high-speed trading networks that involve massive changes in volume trading based on thousands—even, in some cases, tens of thousands—of factors in market conditions. This is going to change the way we buy. This is going to change the way we place an order. This is going to change the way our warehouse restocks itself. This is going to change the way we look at fraud and security. This is going to change the way all kinds of things work—from boarding an airplane to walking into a store.

Today, most of these algorithms are focusing on finding the right match or optimizing behavior. But in the future, they're going to be more sentient. They're going to ask and answer questions. They're going to formulate hypotheses. And this is why we talk about this model being predictive and probabilistic, not deterministic. What we're actually moving toward are models that drive precision decisions.

Self-Learning

The last part of the intention-driven system requires self-learning and cognitive capabilities. What we're talking about here are powerful systems that augment humanity. Digital businesses have cognition. They learn from previous experiences. They analyze failure. Their goal is to augment human decisions and, at some point, automate the mundane and routine but also surface the exceptions that allow for intention-driven systems. This is a convergence of artificial intelligence, dynamic learning, hypothesis generation, and natural language processing.

What we are really doing is trying to figure out how to take all these volumes of data and make them intelligible. If we want to make better decisions, we need this ability to self-learn. Self-learning and cognitive capabilities enable continuous reprogramming. These advances are really a new class of technology that enables human- and machine-guided decisions. This cognition is part of the foundation for what we call augmented humanity, where we're taking our collected insights and data, we're surfacing them in the right time and the right context, and making those decisions. A range of these technologies are now popping up, from facial recognition and human APIs to machine learning, self-learning algorithms.

And that is the promise. We're basically trying to interact more effectively with computing. We're trying to help these machines actually self-learn and understand and interact in a way that makes sense. We're also trying to build deep levels of expertise here. These deep levels of expertise are actually not just in one area. What we're really trying to do is help machines build knowledge, gain a domain, really change the way expert systems move from a hard-coded model to something that's always learning, something that's taking experiences and building on them. Instead of sticking to hard-coded rules, these systems might change over time. This is about the promise of these cognitive systems.

A great example is what's happening at IBM. The company is looking at a world of cognitive computing and thinking about how the human brain and the mind senses and reasons and then making that work inside a computer. It's trying to create these cognitive-computing applications that adjust to experiences and change the way they learn, build knowledge, and ultimately engage with other systems. This allows the systems to act as a decision support system to improve decision making, to improve information distribution based on a limited set of data (or a lot of data), and build those into deep industry expertise.

The challenge here is, we want to get to augmented humanity. We want humans and machines working together. And digital businesses are building these models. Traditionally, the idea behind artificial intelligence is that humans are not in the equation. In fact, humans are completely ruled out. The machines are making their own decisions, doing whatever they're doing. But in cognitive computing, this class of machines is learning from humans and human behavior. Augmented humanity is a part of that. It is creating this level of natural interaction so that we can create feedback loops between machines and humans and sensors. It will allow us to use new techniques to help humans make better decisions. Because while machines can make better automated decisions, humans and machines still need to connect with each other to be most effective.

So the three elements that are most important for delivering on what we're calling intention driven are self-aware sentience, which is the sense and response; predictive probabilistic and not deterministic, which is building smart algorithms; and self-learning and augmented humanity, which is really about our ability to take cognition and bring it to life. This intention-driven mind-set is one of the five key elements for disrupting digital business.

CHAPTER 6

NETWORKED ECONOMIES

ENABLING CO-INNOVATION AND CO-CREATION IN A P2P WORLD

ndividuals and organizations can massively influence the market on their own, but until they plug in to networked economies, they're not going to realize their full potential. It's happening right now. We're really just at the beginning of the chaos and the craziness of what will happen when we connect 75 or 80 billion devices by 2020. We'll be seeing almost three billion people on social networks by 2020. This massive hyperconnectivity is driving what we predict to be somewhere between $70 trillion and $80 trillion in commerce by 2020.

Massive change is happening, and a lot of it is because everything we touch, everything we connect, everything we create results in digital exhaust. This digitalization of everything we touch changes the way we interact, because we can connect with a level of efficiency that we couldn't before, and we can easily bypass any unnecessary friction. These networked economies are disintermediating, or cutting out the middleman, in every market they enter. We're

moving from experiences toward more personalized interactions than ever before.

Networked economies have five characteristics. They
start out with a concept of what we call P2P. This definition is a more evolved version of the peer-to-peer networks
we remember in the first internet boom. These people-
to-people, or point-to-point networks drive the way we
interact on a massive personalized scale. They amplify the
speed, the intensity of signal, and the influence of a person
or organization in that network through force multipliers:
any set of tools, methodologies, advantages, or attributes
that allow you to amplify your effort to produce more output faster, better, and cheaper. The network is a force multiplier, and it's self-interest that helps networks form. This
takes P2P networks from a theoretical value to a meaningful interaction of value exchange and convenience. It
takes away the barriers that create friction in interactions.
In fact, these economies are creating an opportunity to
transform business because of the way these connections
work with one another: they feed off one another and
create different sets of experiences, different sets of interactions. And when the middleman and other barriers are
taken away, you can connect with individuals who actually
know what they're doing. You can connect with systems

that have better pricing information. You can change the way that organizations grow by connecting them directly with decision makers, rather than with trumped-up connections that deliver little in value exchange. This is the transformation piece that helps us change the way organizations use digital to be successful.

So, let's spend some time talking about these P2P networks. We're moving from an era of B to B and B to C to P to P. Remember when most enterprises thought of themselves as B to B or B to C? Many of us still think in those terms; that these models fit what companies or organizations do. But the reality is, they don't. The biggest change today's businesses face is that these traditional, force-fit models of B to B and B to C are being disintermediated by my new definition of P2P. The P2P model, of course, is already in use. It stands for peer to peer, a specific computer networking architecture, but I think of it more broadly, as people-to-people, or point-to-point. It's taking the place of B to B and B to C because business is increasingly being conducted by people who are playing multiple roles or organizations that are acting as individuals.

The driving force behind this shift to people-to-people or point-to-point is from individuals or organizations behaving as individuals would normally act. We already know that the technologies that touch us in our consumer lives are much more powerful than what's happening inside organizations and governments. Individuals are not only empowered by tapping into their own networks to influence outcomes—the power also rests in the hands of many. This is actually happening in the way we connect. Organizations that can tap into these P2P networks are going to accelerate their ability to understand what's happening next. And because individuals make up these organizations, the individuals are much more important than they used to be. These people and their networks are amplifying voices, they're spreading influence. So, you take an effective salesperson or manager or someone in products, and they're actually relying more on their networks outside of the company than the networks inside the company to get things done.

The power of these networks is not just based on how well you're connected, but also on the quality of those connections. With this perspective, it's easy to see that each of the nodes becomes important—who you're connected with, where you're connected. This is critical because it's not how many customers you have or how many Facebook friends that organization has that matters. It's really which customers and which friends actually build that network.

In this new business reality, customers, suppliers, partners, and competitors are all talking to one another. They're all connecting with one another. They're all innovating or creating with one another. They're all advising and—yeah, they're talking about bad experiences or sharing that someone's done a great job. This is the noise in the network, and the noise is only getting louder. The trick is to figure out how to find the right signal-to-noise ratio.

Of course, no business can pay attention to all this chaos, but regardless of what's going on, the reality is that we are seeing a shift in how organizations must interact and build these networked economies with P2P. A divide has emerged between organizations that are taking advantage of P2P networks and those that are waiting to connect. Because the early adopters—the market leaders and fast followers—are winning. The fact that they're connecting to these networks are providing a massive advantage.

Where did P2P come from? Peer-to-peer architecture originally came in when people were trying to exchange files between users. How do you connect two people to share a song or picture or video? Early examples are networks like Napster and LimeWire. People could grab music and files from each other's PCs. Skype routes video calls directly to other computers or smartphones. And

DISRUPTING DIGITAL BUSINESS

these peer-to-peer networks disintermediated any third party that tried to come between two nodes. It meant you didn't have to go through the phone company or another barrier to connect. These traditional P2P networks were the equivalent of passing notes in class without the teacher knowing.

People-to-people networks don't necessarily have to be built around e-technology. Organizations like eBay or Etsy or Lending Club or NeighborGoods or Prosper position themselves at the center of these networks. But they do enable users to lend or sell to one another without involving a bank or retail establishment. As a result, they take advantage of what are called network effects. The more sellers and customers or lenders and borrowers they sign up, the more valuable the service is. The more active those lenders, borrowers, and customers are, the more valuable that service is.

At some of today's P2P enterprises, users actually create the products. As they consume it, they co-innovate and co-create. Look at Facebook and Twitter and Pinterest. These businesses are empty shells of wires without the users talking to one another. The people are the electricity, and the more people on the network, the more power lights up the grid. The information about you, your actions, your preferences, and your network—that's what's important. That's the value. The more interactions, the more data that's collected and analyzed and used to predict future behavior. Even if your business doesn't work like this and isn't being disrupted by businesses that do, these P2P networks are everywhere, and they're affecting your organization. Increasingly, they're how your customers communicate on a daily basis.

You're probably familiar with that reality and more than a little frustrated by it. If all of your customers, partners, suppliers, and competitors aren't just themselves but a part of a network, how do you get anything done? Well, that's actually the point. A big part of why our P2P business environment feels so maddening is that we are not set up to deal with it. The P2P environment is multidimensional. It's complex. It isn't well captured by today's force-fit business processes, which are 2-D. They don't work in a 3-D function, because no one can design a system that can capture every dimension yet. That's why P2P is so important.

Reducing the Unit Cost of Transactions

On the positive side, we're getting better at measuring these interactions and connections. Modern P2P networks generate huge quantities of data that can make relationships and preferences increasingly explicit and transparent, as we've talked about in other parts of this book. A simple network analysis in a P2P network reveals more information about an individual's relationships than face-to-face interactions would have shown in the past. Interest graphs and networks are actually more accurate than what people say up front. Stated preferences may not reflect a person's true behaviors, such as likes or dislikes or transactions or interests. So our ability to predict this behavior and model the complex relationships is what drives a lot of these P2P business models.

What emerges in these P2P networks is an interesting concept, in terms of how we get to a relevant economy of scale (i.e., n economy of scale). In 1937, a British economist, Ronald Coase, argued in his influential article "The Nature of the Firm" that the reason we have firms is because we need to bring economies of scale to business actions that would be too expensive to coordinate in markets. But the idea that big corporations can do things faster and more efficiently has been turned upside down in the past fifteen years, as technology costs have plummeted and businesses have become more consumer focused. In fact, a four-person company can now do business on a level that would have needed a fifty-person company just a few years ago. This is happening at a dizzying rate. I even look at my own company, Constellation Research. What we can achieve with twenty people is much more effective today than what two hundred people could have done, say, five years ago. It's because of how we're connected. It's the way we can communicate. It's the way we tap into our networks. These P2P networks actually allow us to scale up and compete with a two-hundred-person company. It sounds crazy, but with today's P2P model, we are actually set up in a way that we don't have to hire all the experts that a large firm does. Instead, we can use the power of our networks to recreate similar access and levels of services for our clients. We can create alliances with individuals to actually compete with existing organizations. And we can do it without having to build the same level of infrastructure and scale to retain those individuals. We can build them and retain them in a virtual way. That's the power of these P2P networks. They empower organizations to compete and to change the way we co-create and co-innovate. This idea is new, and it is transforming business models. We move from who we partner with to whom we co-innovate and co-create with.

So, what we're talking about now is how networks are force multipliers. It's the networks, stupid. In other words, if everyone is part of a network, the network then amplifies our actions. But you can't ignore a network. Ignoring a network is like playing an electric guitar with the amplifier turned off. How we bring these networks together matters, as they are critical in building a business community. We have to bet on these networks to gain influence and increase market share.

There are five types of networks. P2P business environments can be connected at an individual level, as direct teams, as partners and alliances, as extended value chains, and through external advocate ecosystems.

- **Individuals.** What does it mean to be connected at the individual level? These modern P2P networks allow individuals to exert influence in a way that only organizations could put forth in the past. A person can tweet as easily as a corporation can. A person can tap into her network and recruit as easily or even more effectively than a corporation can. A blog is a publishing tool in the hands of anyone who wants to use it. Bringing collections of individuals together to create a network in the digital environment will result in monumental changes.

- **Direct teams.** We can also create networks as direct teams. Employees and team members not only bring their personal networks to an organization, but expand the organization's presence in added directions and sectors. Make sure adding employees expands your firm's network presence instead of simply reinforcing it.

- **Partners and alliances.** A company can expand and strengthen its networks through agreements and business development relationships with others. Also in this category are direct sales programs, such as Tupperware and Mary Kay.

- **Extended value chains.** Firms exert influence over each of their business processes, from manufacturing and supply to distribution, sales, and marketing. Apple's ability to flex its production and supply chain to create mass production while driving demand through its stores to generate the highest profitability per square foot is an example of influence in action over this type of network.

- **External advocate ecosystems.** The converted and curious. Who out in the world has got your company's religion and where do they commune? Examples include support forums, online communities, and fan/supporter organizations.

Force Multipliers

The term "force multiplier"—again, any set of tools, advantages, or attributes that allow you to amplify your effort to produce more output faster, better, and cheaper—comes from the military. A machine gun allows a shooter to deliver more firepower than he would be able to shoot with a rifle. In other words, it's a force multiplier. If you're an organization and you want to grow, and you're only reaching one customer at a time, or one market at a time, or one partnership at a time, you're not going to grow fast enough to be competitive—especially with larger players that have full infrastructure in the marketplace.

But force multipliers create disintermediation that allows a smaller organization to not only scale up to serve existing opportunities, but also to create opportunities that a small organization could not have supported in the past. Think about Pebble Technologies and what they had to do to raise funds with Kickstarter. Using the force multiplier of Kickstarter, Pebble quickly built a community of investors that it didn't know it had—individual users who contributed $100 or $150 at a time. This helped them raise a ridiculous amount of money to go build a watch, literally an LCD watch. This is what we're talking about: tapping into the power of networks. Tapping into the power of P2P. That's the force multiplier.

There are a lot of force multipliers out there, but I've settled on seven types: network sharing, user-generated content, crowdsourcing, flash networks, dedicated advocates, situation awareness, and predictive hotspotting. These sound abstract, so let's define each one:

- **Network sharing.** Network sharing allows users to share ideas and information very quickly. The speed and reach that we have today in social networks such as Facebook or LinkedIn or Twitter make network sharing an important force multiplier that is designed to facilitate communications at the node-to-node, person-to-person level.

- **User-generated content.** User-generated content creates a force multiplier by allowing the audience and the community to provide content. This multiplier includes not just content but also user-generated connections. So, we're able to use these user-generated capabilities inside an existing network to provide input, to design the next product, to think about how you go about, say, reviewing a restaurant. We're actually seeing this approach in action now. It's a new way for reviews to work, for ideas to come together. Yelp, Angie's List, and other companies provide professional services and ratings in this arena.

- **Crowdsourcing.** Crowdsourcing basically involves convincing other people to help you do stuff. The idea is not new. For example, in Mark Twain's novel *Tom Sawyer*, Tom convinces the neighborhood children to help him whitewash a fence, simply for the honor of being part of it. Technology enables crowdsourcing to deliver a high force multiplier by outsourcing both simple and complex work to a low- to no-cost model. There are different ways to influence and reward people within this model. The tasks have to be small enough and nimble enough that large groups can do them in little time. A great example of this is the web-based crowdsourcing marketplace Amazon Mechanical Turk. Another is the SETI project, where folks are aiding the nonprofit SETI Institute in trying to search for extraterrestrial life by providing their excess computing power to support the effort. Crowdsourcing has other uses than labor. Organizations such as Kickstarter and Y Combinator provide crowdsourced funding. Indiegogo is another example of that. A design marketplace like 99design gives you access to a talent network. And there's oDesk, where projects can be proposed and talent brought together. Spigot is another company that creates a forum for crowdsourced ideas. The point is, you've got this array of ways to crowdsource, not only to raise money but to generate labor and ideas.

- **Flash networks.** Flash mobs were pioneered by magazine editor Bill Wasik as a social experiment and, to a large extent, a joke. But modern flash networks can actually be serious attempts to create pop-up networks. An example is the pop-up store that appears in the middle of a large crowd or event and then goes away afterward. It comes from a network's ability to generate interest and attention quickly to bring people together. Here's an example. In March 2011, Apple created a pop-up store in Austin, Texas, to sell the new iPad. The choice of location was far from accidental: it was three blocks away from the music and film festival South by Southwest. That means 20,000 technologists—media and digital influencers—were next door. So the ability to create a flash network on the fly is a massive force multiplier for being able to address a need. If you see massive demand for, say, merchandise from the Disney movie *Frozen*, how do you create something really quickly to capitalize on a trend, and of course, bring it back down when that trend loses steam? That's where flash networks come in.

- **Dedicated advocates.** Consider advocates to be a step up from customer engagement. These are dedicated fans, dedicated partners who believe in your brand, your cause, your mission, your product. Advocates are the ones who talk about you. They refer people in. They answer questions on your forums. They write a blog about your organization. They do all this for free. Advocates are typically not paid, but they take their engagement with you and the relationship very seriously. As force multipliers, advocates are the first folks that support—and also may be the first to criticize—what you're trying to accomplish.

- **Situation awareness.** This idea was pioneered by industrial engineer Mica Endsley. The technique is often applied to what we call time-dependent situations, such as aviation, or emergency services, or even the battlefield. Situation awareness means that your network has the right information at the right time to make speedy and informed decisions, the ability to go from reaction to prediction. The point is to connect and get from reaction to prediction very, very quickly and create a force multiplier so that you always have the right information at the right time and you can react and jump into something before everyone else.

- **Predictive hotspotting.** A force multiplier taken to the highest level is predictive hotspotting. This is the holy grail. In a digital network, in a digital world, the goal is to find out, Will something happen in the near future? And how is it going to happen in the near future? To what degree will that be true? Organizations are running streams of data through algorithms to make better predictions in terms of how they deploy their people, how they attack a market, and we're seeing these all over. Law enforcement agencies use predictive hotspotting to decide on staffing, where to put police cars, where to predict a crime. Health-care providers are using hotspotting to figure out which clinics and which neighborhoods are going to be more useful to the local population and for determining treatment patterns and staffing needs. We're seeing predictive hotspotting as a force multiplier because how do we convert all the data inside the system to the decisions piece we talked about earlier? How do we take these insights and ask the questions and predict what's going to happen next?

Incentives

How do we appeal to people's self-interest? Because in a networked economy, you've got to align with self-interest, otherwise you don't have an economy. Incentives are worthless if they do not come from an understanding of what people want or need, so you have to listen before you incentivize, or your offerings will fall on deaf ears. Incentives also come from the other party's self-interest. If you don't align with that self-interest, you'll find yourself quite alone.

If you want to be successful, you need to incentivize people or points, not organizations. You incentivize the node so that you can actually connect. Let's face it: people are inherently self-interested. There's a big difference between saying that and saying they are selfish. If you're selfish, you give yourself priority above all others. But being self-interested means that you are aware of and clear about your preferences, and you act on them. There's an attraction to what you find interesting. Most folks are ashamed to admit this because by admitting that we have preferences we open ourselves up to easy characterization and stereotyping. If I say I prefer X, it's easy to assume I don't care for Y, and few of us like coming off as contrary, argumentative, and maybe worst of all, selfish: "I prefer X and don't care about anything else but me and my love of X." But to truly understand what people are interested in and how they're motivated, we have to observe their behavior. We have to listen. We have to identify the patterns from what they do and what they say they do, and we need to get to the root cause to understand their motivation, because that's how we incentivize people. We have to understand that core need, that core self-interest, that drives someone.

So what's the right way to incentivize? This is where we put together user profiles and organizational profiles based on self-interest and achievement drivers. For example, an employer who awards the employee of the month a parking space in a metropolitan area may have the wrong prize if most folks actually take public transit to work. Great idea, great concept, but wrong reward, and you're not going to get a lot of response. If the organization is an environmental nonprofit, a parking spot might not fly for different but equally powerful reasons. So, how does our imaginary employer know what its employees want? How does our imaginary organization know exactly what customers are looking for and how to get them incentivized? And how do you figure out how to get this information without being invasive or overly direct? This is really the question.

We've got to think about how to create appealing non-monetary incentives. A 2011 Constellation Research study showed that professionals and creative employees are motivated 41 percent more by nonmonetary incentives than they are by monetary ones. The research looked at decisions employees made, not at their verbalized or surveyed preferences. These findings jibe with a larger body of current research that indicates employees are significantly more motivated by how meaningful their work is, and the mastery and purpose that they have over it, than they are by traditional incentive systems. The point is that a system of carrots and sticks or pats on the back for good work and "wags of a finger" for bad work as a relic of a centralized twentieth-century industrial economy doesn't reflect these P2P networks, and it is definitely less relevant in a P2P business environment where self-interest assumes center stage. Many of us have seen this in Daniel Pink's 2011 book *Drive: The Surprising Truth Behind What Motivates Us*. But there's more than employees involved here. Incentives for customers in the market they represent are often nonmonetary too.

These nonmonetary incentives can be divided into three important categories: recognition, access, and impact.

- **Recognition.** In this category, it's badges and points and loyalty cards and leader boards and customer-of-the-month plaques. These are all examples of recognition, or how a company rewards customers for increased levels of involvement. Our research indicates that 15 percent to 25 percent of early adopters in a community will engage with a company for recognition. Everybody wants their day. Everyone wants their fifteen minutes of fame. And more than 60 percent want further participation influence through recognition. Recognition is about having someone say, "Hey, we noticed you." And that's important. That nonmonetary act of just being noticed by someone—that is, being perceived as important to that other individual in the network—creates a lot of interest and facilitates the process of getting to an engagement.

- **Access.** Access refers to privileges that more-engaged individuals get over less-engaged people in that node. So, in the P2P network, many organizations will allow engaged customers special roles as product testers and moderators. These people get to do things that no one else gets to do because of what they've accomplished or what the company sets as the reward. One classic example is how elite-status frequent flyers are granted entry into a club room. In a consumer environment, this may mean that you get to see a product. You get to be at the product launch before anyone else. You get to test the product and connect with it before anybody else gets to. In an employee situation, it might mean you get access to a special set of perks that no one else gets. Roughly 10 percent of a community will see access as an intrinsic motivator. More than 80 percent will be influenced by a desire for greater access.

- **Impact.** This is the degree to which a customer or employee may influence a future direction of a product or company. In a P2P network, by definition, impact is only attained by the most-committed users. In a P2P network, only a few people are actually driving a lot of the conversation, but they're influencing a lot of other folks. Not everybody takes an active role: organizations on average see just 27 percent of their network members as fully engaged members. Of the engaged members, 13 percent drive 80 percent of the influence. Only 5 percent to 10 percent are "super-users." These are people who want to build a better product. These are people who want to co-innovate and co-create with you for free. Not monetarily.

They want to build something. They want to change something. These are very, very valuable folks in the network, especially in a P2P network. And it's essential to identify them.

The challenge of building these incentives is, Who are we creating value for? And for what? How do we determine what next actions we want to incentivize and the relative value to the recipients? Would dinner with the CEO of the company be worth more than the opportunity to audition for the next TV commercial? A smart marketer knows that the answer is almost always, "It depends." And yet the marketer can't march into a strategy meeting and throw "It depends" on the whiteboard. But then, how do you create a kind of measurability around these incentives, and how can you predict what the customer market will do? And so, and this is the important thing, we have to think about the relative value to the other person in the P2P network. The other person in the P2P network is what's key. This is how you drive these transactions. This is what we're trying to match to take friction out of the system.

That brings us to the conversation around convenience. And in these P2P networks, let's be real: laziness is human, so we have to take advantage of it. If you pave the path of least resistance, it will be easier for your customers to engage with you. That means you have to conduct business on your customers' terms. They aren't always right, but in a P2P world, these are the only terms that matter. You can educate them. You can change their behavior over time, but at this point, you have to conduct business based on what your customers want.

Any time you have friction, you get loss. And what we want here in convenience is to drive down friction. But if people are inherently lazy, organizations are even lazier. In fact, most of us will stick it out in a bad situation because bad situations seem easier than the work required to change them. As customers, we will only switch options if it's easier or more convenient. But easy does not mean it's right for us. Easy just means it's easier. In a P2P world where an entire network of options and choices are a click away, or a connection away, or a button away, easy is ultimately the only factor that matters. Small wonder then that we've labeled an entire field of design as "user experience." User experience can refer to how comfortable the seat on an airplane is or how close the tables are in a restaurant. But primarily it means how quickly can customers complete their intended actions with a minimum of time, confusion, and holdup? How do we make it easy for folks? How do we drive down to this point that people are ultimately lazy, and if you can make it easy for them, they will do what you want them to do?

If you can streamline a process and eliminate the barriers, you can achieve a frictionless experience, and this is what we're trying to do. The concept of a frictionless experience is one in which barriers are removed that take away from the experience. As you can imagine, this is completely subjective: one hotel guest may want a soft alarm clock to nudge him out of sleep while a business traveler might want a blaring, lazybones alarm to get the day started. Frictionless experiences are by nature customer focused. Frictionless experiences allow people to set their preferences and make it easy. So, for example, let's take a coffee shop. If it remembers your top three orders and allows you to order on your way there, pay by mobile app, and just pick it up in line as you get there, you've reduced the friction caused by the need to stand in line to order and then wait to pay and deal with cash and change. Instead, the only experience you have is waiting for the coffee to be handed to you. A coffee shop may want to have customers wait in line so they'll buy additional items, however. Because they can actually sell more items, and they can upsell on the fly if people are waiting in line. But if certain customers want speed, a frictionless, order-ahead experience may be ultimately both to their benefit and to the benefit of the coffee shop. The shop can process more customers faster with the convenience approach. The customers perceive the shop as understanding their time constraints, and an organization that creates that perception—that convenience equals anticipating a customer's needs—can not only predict but influence customer behavior. Are we willing to trade some of that convenience and optimization for more revenue, instead of actually trying to upsell something? This is what we're trying to do.

So how do you design for this kind of convenience? Well, there are different mantras. One is "Keep it simple, stupid." Ease of use and simplicity ultimately trump complexity. Give it to me with no manuals, no training. The offering should be easy to learn, repeatable with minimal effort, and not be complex. The simpler and more efficient the design, the more customers see the organization as being on their side, and the more likely they will be to switch if they have to. Faster means taking out process inefficiencies. How do we cut through the red tape? How do we take out something that's actually a barrier? How do we take out a middleman? Faster doesn't mean lessened or reduced experience. Faster is about being first. Faster is about not waiting in line. Faster is just about being fast.

Beginning with the end in mind is how we understand the customer's motivation. Solutions must solve the core problem, not simply address the symptom. And so we're getting to "purpose built." Purpose built becomes more important than general and vague. When we're trying to drive down friction and make things more convenient, the more something is purpose built, the more likely it's going to relate to someone. We have to get to specificity.

And you want to turn it into a verb. When you make a copy, you Xerox it. To search, you Google. Or Bing. Success comes when you've set expectations on the outcome and what you deliver becomes a simple action verb. This is going back to the brand promise. When we deliver a promise or an experience, we turn it into a verb, and people actually equate that verb with a convenience. We equate that verb to the action, that brand promise. That's really where we want to go.

While customers aren't always right, you do have to conduct business on your customers' terms. And this is why the convenience element is so important in these networks. If you add friction to the process while a competitor is reducing friction, you're going to lose nine out of ten times. Convenience has to be defined around that P2P network's point of view. Do you design your store so there are only staff people behind the counter? Or do you make sure every clerk standing can actually check you out? If it takes someone five minutes to wait in line, versus five seconds to check out, guess who wins? If you've seen an Apple store versus a CompUSA—if you remember those—you know the answer. Convenience wins, and this is why it's so important in these networks.

Freemium

In the area around self-interest, we have to talk about value exchange. If you're exchanging fair value, you actually conduct a transaction. A great view of this is how the concept of freemium works in networked economies. In his 2009 book *Free: The Future of Radical Price*, author and former *Wired* editor Chris Anderson explains, "Freemium is the inverse of the traditional free sample. Instead of giving away 1 percent of your product to sell 99 percent, you give away 99 percent of your product to sell 1 percent. The reason this makes sense is that for digital products, where the marginal cost is close to zero, the 99 percent costs you little and allows you to reach a huge market. So the 1 percent you convert is 1 percent of a big number."

In the enterprise software world I came from, organizations often pay up to $5,000 a person for a software license. If you have 500 employees, that means $2.5 million in software costs. On top of that, companies also pay 20 percent a year for software maintenance and support—which means another $2.5 million every five years. Thus, enterprise software is a very expensive proposition for customers and a very lucrative value proposition for software publishers. However, by dealing with only the very top of the market, those same software publishers have put a natural limit on the number of customers they can reach.

This has opened up areas of the enterprise software market to companies like Atlassian, Box, Evernote, Hootsuite, and Yammer that work on freemium models. Instead of paying millions for content management and social software, an organization can start with the basic feature set and work its way to premium pricing as its needs grow. The premium offer often starts with additional features that add value. These could be the ability to share a file, gain better reporting or metrics, increase flexibility and control, and receive more storage.

Evernote subscribers gain supersized uploads, better security, offline access, and top priority support. Yammer customers get better support, Microsoft SharePoint integration, and Microsoft Office 365 integration as they increase their price per user. The results show how many users are willing to pay for value. Evernote converts 3 percent of its free users to paid membership. Yammer claims 19 percent freemium-to-premium conversion.

An offshoot of this model is Box. Box allows individuals to join for free, while charging enterprises. About 8 percent of individual end users have converted their organizations to become paid enterprise customers. As you can see, this is networked economies in action. Paid enterprise Box users get more storage, more users, and more collaborative features. Another offshoot is Atlassian, which takes freemium to another level with cause marketing. Atlassian takes a micro payment for its software and donates the money toward a charity or cause. In 2010, the company donated $500,000 of $2.5 million in revenue to the charity Room to Read.

Despite the sexiness of these models, there are challenges. Let's take a look at the newspaper industry, which has been decimated around the world. Though a few markets, such as India and Brazil, have seen subscriber growth in the print form, at most papers advertising revenues have fallen as printing and transportation costs have risen.

One solution is to implement a paywall. A common argument against paywalls is that open access brings a larger audience, and that requires more advertising revenue. In a world where readers share content and links through social networks, the theory is sound. The more free access, the greater the sharing, the more eyeballs, and the higher the rates, right? Unfortunately, online rates are only a fraction of print ad rates. Newspapers and other print media have not made up the difference in volume.

In 1995, the *Wall Street Journal* made a controversial decision when it introduced the *Wall Street Journal* online edition—and kept it behind a paywall. To critics' surprise, the *Journal* had signed up 200,000 online subscribers by 1997. The *Journal* is now the United States' largest newspaper by circulation, at 2.3 million in 2012—of which 800,000 were digital-only subscriptions.

What seemed a crazy idea in 1997 has now emerged as a trend. Eleven out of the twenty major newspapers in the United States have announced or have plans to implement paywalls, despite readers being accustomed to "free" news.

In March 2011, the *New York Times* unveiled its paywall. By the end of 2012, the *Times* was earning more from circulation than from advertising, helped by the growth in digital subscriptions. Of $768.3 million in circulation revenue in 2012, 12 percent came from digital.

The success of the *Wall Street Journal* and the *New York Times* stems from the high-quality journalism they produce and the brand perception that the average, informed reader is missing something in going without them. That reader probably works in business or finance in the case of the *Wall Street Journal*. In the case of the *New York Times*, the company is trading on its century-and-a-half-long reputation as the world's news source of record.

In both cases, the audience is both consuming quality journalism and perhaps participating in discussions, circulating articles, and arming themselves for upcoming dialogue with their family, colleagues, and friends. In the rarified air at the summit of the newspaper industry, the principles of P2P are working and are at scale.

Though the average local paper may have its community in place, its offerings may not be seen as indispensable and its readership might not be large enough to support the resources necessary to generate enough premium content to justify erecting a paywall.

Even a paper as large and prestigious as the *Washington Post* has resisted. Though seen as a national paper, the print edition is not nationally distributed, despite the fact that 90 percent of its digital traffic comes from outside the DC metro area. A decision to implement a paywall in 2012 was halted due to reader and industry outcries.

To be sure, some old-line media companies have succeeded in monetizing nonjournalism areas of their business. The Washington Post Company owns the Stanley Kaplan education business. Atlantic Media, publishers of the *Atlantic* magazine, have a burgeoning live-event business and a series of web portals that serve well-off niche sectors of its readership.

The debate over paywalls and journalism is far from over. Yet the rather spotty history of success demonstrates the difficulty of executing freemium models well—what offerings, for how much and to whom, the DNA of value.

A forcing function in the networked economy is how much folks will trade for convenience. And this is where monetary and nonmonetary value exchange comes in. Privacy is a great example of this, and there is no better example than Facebook, where value exchange is all about trading privacy for convenience

Facebook understands convenience and networked economies. It is the poster child for this idea, and it started from day one. Facebook gets its users to share massive amounts of information about themselves from photos, comments, actions, and interactions—and it gets them to share by making it insanely convenient.

As of August 2012, Facebook's content consisted of over 2.7 billion likes, 300 million photos, and 2.5 billion pieces of user-generated content—500 terabytes of data in all. This is all information that users willingly provide to Facebook and that Facebook then uses to continually make its processes easier. Through facial recognition, Facebook can conveniently identify your friends in each photo. Your likes have been categorized so you see what your friends like as well. The more you put in, the easier the user experience becomes.

Along the way, Facebook is getting better and better at predicting what you'll do next and what you might want to spend money on. With that insight in hand, Facebook can get advertisers to pay millions to influence users' next set of actions and decisions.

Caveat emptor reigns when people pay nothing to use a product in a world where *they* are the product. The convenience of Facebook and the free nature of the product means all your data, your preferences, your network, and your actions are owned by Facebook, to mine and sell to advertisers as it chooses. Facebook now knows more about you than your government, your closest family member, or maybe even you yourself.

This all sounds creepy, perhaps even disgusting. But Facebook is not the IRS or the Social Security Administration. No one is required to participate, and those who want to may conduct their relationships without ever logging in to Facebook. But Facebook's very ubiquity makes opting out difficult and less socially acceptable—the digital-age version of not having a telephone or indoor plumbing.

It's been argued repeatedly that Facebook should make it easier for users to control which of their data is shared with whom. That level of difficulty (high to too high) reveals the company's intimate understanding of the law of convenience. Facebook knows that just a few extra hurdles, and its users won't bother. Why? Because Facebook makes it too easy to get too many tasks of digital-age life done. And the fact that it charges nothing for use raises the question, "Well just what should Facebook be doing to make money?" The company is simply the largest example of what we already know about the space it pioneered: a service that charges nothing for its use views its users as the product.

Will those users stop trading privacy for convenience? And at what point? The law of convenience runs deep.

Noted technology industry guru Tim O'Reilly argues that "Facebook is creating more value than they capture." He's right. The trade-offs between privacy and convenience will continue, but convenience usually wins.

Privacy is not dead. It's only dead if we choose not to make it convenient.

Co-Innovation and Co-Creation in the Platform

When one mentions General Electric, one normally thinks of a company that was the poster child of the industrial age. However, GE is rapidly applying disrupting digital business through its software embedded in its machinery as well as through the Internet of Things. But going it alone is not enough for GE to succeed. Early on, GE realized that the company could not put together all the components, connections, and technology for large-scale projects on its own.

GE formed the Industrial Internet Consortium to bring together partners to co-innovate and co-create new business models and deliver deep industry expertise. Partners include obvious system integrators such as Accenture,

Deloitte, IBM, and Tech Mahindra. Technology members even include potential competitors such as Fujitsu, Mitsubishi Electric, and Toshiba.

The power of the networked economy is stronger than the competitive forces. While GE uses its proprietary Predix big-data capture and analysis platform as the backbone, the product is built on open source technologies such as R and Spring. That open source component enables partners to extend capabilities with their own intellectual property. The result is a collection of what GE calls Predictivity Solutions, which are driving $1 billion in annual revenue.

CHAPTER 7

LIVING AND WORKING IN AN ERA OF DIGITAL BUSINESS

et's cut to the chase and get started. Over the past two years or so, my company, Constellation Research, has interviewed, studied, or assisted more than a hundred market leaders and fast followers that are working to create a digital transformation strategy. We've learned that regardless of industry size or company or geography, these early adopters take five common steps to be successful in an era of digital business:

1. They design new experiences and business models that reflect brand authenticity.

2. They develop and nourish a culture of digital DNA.

3. They apply new technologies to existing infrastructure.

4. They move from gut-driven decisions to data-driven ones.

5. They attract new partners to co-create and co-innovate on their platforms.

In each case, these steps provide the foundation to not only transform business models through digital, but also to reinvent the brand promise.

1. Design New Experiences

Let's start with talking about designing new experiences. The goal here is to use digital as an opportunity to craft new experiences. Customers seek outcomes and experiences, but most organizations are still selling products and services. Awesome experiences are now the expected norm—and companies can't afford to ignore that.

Success in digital business models comes from reinforcing the brand promise and promoting the brand mythology. New business models must be part of the new experiences. We see the shift in three areas addressed in earlier chapters: mass personalization at scale, big data business models, and augmented humanity. These provide a starting point toward designing a new digital experience. Early adopters all have applied concepts in design thinking from the beginning.

Mass personalization at scale is the design point of digital businesses. The delivery of a customer segment of one defines success. This shift from analog to digital systems includes a progression from systems of transaction, of engagement, of experience, and of mass personalization at scale. That first shift gave us automation-driven efficiencies. But what we're doing right now in the digital world is achieving mass personalization at scale. These systems start with an outcome-driven design point: solve the delivery—individual P2P on a massive scale that allows us to craft personalized conversation, interface with human APIs, and enable P2P networks.

Old-line industries in the analog world can redesign experiences and bring this information onto new user experiences. Context engines can cut the hype of information overload and deliver relevant information in real time and at the right time. New payment technologies, digital wallets, and personal cloud functionality can take friction out of the purchase process. The goal is to take these technological advancements and craft new experiences.

So how do we take these isolated networks and move them into a connected world of sensor-based and analytic ecosystems that take advantage of all this data? In both the consumer and enterprise worlds, smart machines and wearables are driving new types of sensors, and they're adding to the mix of data that's available to create new insights. We're estimating there will be as many as 200 million smart wearables by 2017. These products will include bracelets, watches, eyewear, clothing, and other devices with sensors. Data from equipment, such as automobiles, medical devices, and household appliances, as well as power generators and building management systems, will give us an opportunity to improve efficiencies, create new business models, and identify new usage patterns.

For example, my house should know that I like it to be 72 degrees when I get home. My car can tell the house when I'm thirty minutes away, and the house—based on my past preferences and actions—should adjust the temperature on its own. This is the kind of stuff that we're talking about. The car is connected to the house. The house is connected to a temperature sensor. The house also learns that when I come back from the gym, I like the house at 65 degrees. This is the AI associated with the house looking at the pattern of my behaviors. These systems are not only communicating with one another, they're also interfacing with people, overtly and covertly. This Internet of Things is moving from abstract concept to living and breathing machine—the machine mesh network interfaced with humanity.

What comes next is augmenting humanity and creating powerful, yet static cognitive systems that augment human decisions. Cognitive computing is more than a new category. These systems represent a new class of technology, converging artificial intelligence, facial recognition, human APIs, natural language processing, dynamic learning, and hypothesis generation to render vast quantities of data intelligible to improve both human- and machine-guided decisions. The ability to self-learn lets these systems continuously reprogram. Augmenting humanity means that our collective insights and data can be served up at the right time and in the right context.

What does this mean in terms of new experiences? It means if you're a lawyer, you can ask a machine, What are fifteen other cases like this and what were the outcomes? What should I look for? As an accountant, you can look for similar types of tax risks or audit risks that could occur. If you're a physician you could ask, Are there other patients with a similar type of genetic makeup? With these specific drug interactions? What other cases have you seen like this? And all this information and all these answers come up. These are brand-new experiences. We're actually creating new opportunities and ways for people to interact. You can even just go and talk to a machine and say,

"Look, I want to fly to San Francisco, to New York, and then to London on these dates. These are the features I like. What are the available flights?" These integrative experiences will create a huge shift in the way we work.

2. Develop a Culture of Digital DNA

Success begins at the top. Digital transformation requires strong leaders who are not afraid of dips in share prices, cannibalizing existing markets, and identifying new approaches. Organizations have to assess their innate ability to thrive in a digital business environment and nurture digital artisans.

What are digital artisans? They are a class of individuals who blend the intelligence of quant jocks with the co-innovation skills of creatives. We've got to figure out how to thrive in this digital business environment, and doing that means looking beyond those who deliver hard science and engineering prowess but also beyond those who can co-innovate and co-create on demand. Consequently, organizations are rethinking the attributes of digital business and what the emerging candidate for chief digital officer should embody. We're now seeing a rise in demand for the digital artisans that are required for this type of organizational transformation. There's a new war for talent, and it's going to focus on attracting, developing, and retaining these digital artisans. Concurrently, a market will develop for those who can spread the digital business gospel and infuse digital artistry into organizations.

While there are many attributes a digital business should embody, there are seven building blocks that define these digital artisans, who embody the digital DNA required for success. Together, they spell "artisan":

Authenticity. You need to stay true to the organization's mythology and brand.

Relevancy. Deliver contextual personalization at scale.

Transparency. Operate with an understanding that everything will eventually become public.

Intelligence. Adapt self-learning systems that anticipate users' needs.

Speed. Infuse responsiveness into digital time.

Analysis. Democratize decision making with all types of data, but do it in a way that's visual and helps people make decisions.

Nonconformism. Espouse disruption and the creation of new ideas. This is more than thinking outside the box. This is acting toward that, and facilitating a culture that delivers on this.

As we think about developing this talent, we also need to create diversity in thinking. This corresponds to more than race or age. We need a balance of thought. An organization with several scientists should be balanced out by a recruitment of design thinking experts, philosophers, or anthropologists. In an organization with too many thinkers, balance out the team with those who can execute.

This is also about digital proficiency. We're talking about five generations of workers. Not Millennials, Gen Yers, Gen Xers, Baby Boomers, and the post-war generation. Rather, the shift to digital business is five generations defined in terms of where you work, when you work, how you work, what you work on, and why you work. These definitions have been completely disrupted in the digital world. These five generations of workers have different people-centric values that have to be addressed, and the segmentation describes how digitally proficient people are with digital technologies and culture. The five generations include:

Digital natives. These are people who grew up with the internet, and they are comfortable engaging in all digital channels. Digital natives could be ninety years old, or they could be seventeen. They are very comfortable with technology, and the way they communicate and interact, as well as their expectations, are built around this technology.

Digital immigrants. These are people who have crossed the chasm to the digital world. They were forced into engagement and digital channels, and they're navigating between analog and digital all the time.

Digital voyeurs. These are people who recognize the shift to digital and observe it at arm's length. They're not against it. They know it's happening, but they haven't dipped their toe into the water.

Digital holdouts. These are people who resist the shift to digital, ignoring its impact. They're scared.

They're not ready to jump in. They're happy with their life as it is.

Digitally disengaged. These are people who were involved in digital technology early, but they've given up on it. They're scared post-Snowden. They're obsessed with erasing their digital exhaust.

Let's see how this works. A digital immigrant takes notes on paper and transcribes them onto a computer. A digital native just takes notes on her computer. A digital voyeur keeps a notebook and doesn't even bother to transcribe to digital, and a digital holdout doesn't even bother with the computer. The digitally disengaged individual is out there trying to erase every single document he's ever put on the web.

Another way to look at it is how you wake up in the morning. If you wake up to an alarm clock, you're probably a digital holdout. Waking up to a watch could make you a digital voyeur. Using a wake-up call could make you digitally disengaged. Waking up to a smartphone makes you a digital native, or maybe a digital immigrant. I have an alarm clock, the same alarm clock I've had since second grade, which I use at home, but I don't use an alarm clock at a hotel. Where does that put me? But the point here is to show you how these five generations of digital proficiency work and come into play.

3. Apply New Technologies to Existing Infrastructure

Going digital doesn't mean a wholesale replacement of existing technologies. It doesn't mean just putting up a mobile front or adding a social collaboration feature to a process. The convergence of mobile, social, cloud, analytics, big data, and communications is just one starting point. Adding sensors to old machinery provides data in context. Mobilizing mainframe data for use in analytics delivers new experiences and provides insight into new opportunities. Bringing external data to internal systems creates new patterns that provide better data for testing out new business models. You want to use this opportunity to rethink your technology strategy, so you can align business objectives with digital transformation. It's not about just adding one technology to change how things are working. It's deeper than that.

A digital reference architecture is emerging. There are eight factors to consider in developing these next-generation platforms, and they align back with many other elements I've been talking about.

1. **Brand authenticity remains paramount.** Trust and transparency will drive brand authenticity in digital systems. Every touch point, every click, and every sensor fired will either enhance or damage the brand. The cumulative set of interactions determines brand presence, influence, and value. Digital systems must not only monitor but also apply corrective actions to ensure brand authenticity. Technologies may include sensor-filled and analytical ecosystems tied to advanced brand monitoring networks. For example, brand monitoring will move from reactive to proactive intervention with brand goals driving overall customer engagement strategies.

2. **Right-time contextual relevancy drives engagement.** Context is king in digital. While real-time delivery is emphasized, real time creates more noise and fewer signals in a world deluged by data. Achievement of contextual relevancy will require systems to capture, process, and publish contextual elements such as role, relationship,

ownership, business process, channel, time, location, weather, sentiment, and even intent. For instance, a conference attendee could note the most interesting individuals or trade show booths from their mobile app or augmented reality device as they enter the show floor. They could even see personal LinkedIn profiles or the latest news using a video version of Shazam.

3. **Probabilistic business processes enable personalized journeys.** The world of forced-fit deterministic business processes built on the best practices of yesterday and applied to today's engagement journeys often fail. Digital platforms must support choose-your-own-adventure journeys. These probabilistic models orchestrate composable APIs and customer journeys to allow users to customize their experiences. Technologies move to advanced complex-event-processing engines, advanced business process management, and intelligent workflows. Imagine the ability to shop in-store, buy online, return by mail, schedule installation, and apply a refund to a gift card anytime, anywhere, and in any order.

4. **Augmented humanity improves decisions.** A convergence of artificial intelligence, natural language processing, dynamic learning, and hypothesis generation renders vast quantities of data intelligible to help humans make better decisions. The ability to self-learn enables continuous reprogramming. These advancements represent a new class of technology to enable human and machine-guided decisions. Cognitive computing, self-learning systems, and knowledge bases drive augmented humanity, where the sum of our collective insights and data can be served up at the right time in the right context. Technologies include facial recognition, human APIs, machine learning, natural language processing and self-learning algorithms. The goal is to democratize data to democratize decision making inside digital systems for all types of stakeholders.

5. **Access versus ownership of information changes design points.** Many studies state that 90 percent of the world's data was created in the last two years. Constellation estimates that by 2020, 60

percent of an organization's mission-critical data will reside outside of its firewalls and owned secure environments. Add the mash-up of data points from insight networks, and most organizations must design systems to rapidly access, process, refine, and distribute insights from external systems. Technologies include data preparation, data governance, data integration, data distribution, context engines, and broadcast networks. Users can expect situational awareness capabilities from mash-ups of insights.

6. **Engagement driven by self-interest creates frictionless value exchange.** Improved user experiences and value exchange frameworks come together to create a market for ease of self-interested experiences. This design element drives friction and transaction costs from the user experience while creating a mechanism that enables users to trade value elements for convenience. Expect more fine-tuned and explicit trading networks that are self-interested and emphasize convenience. Technologies include bionic APIs, trading networks, gamification models, payment

systems, and identity networks. Digital wallets such as Google Wallet and Apple Pay are examples where users trade identity and payment information for convenience.

7. **Digital business models provide new opportunities.** New business models must focus on delivery at the smallest incremental unit. These unit-cost business models must also support aggregated bundles customized to the individual. Digital business models also aggregate, refine, and broker insights. The value of insight networks will enable organizations to drive 20 percent of their revenue from insights by 2020. Big data business models are an example where organizations can provide the content, serve as an enabler, or play the role of the insight network.

8. **Networked ecosystems deliver digital scale in the market.** Success in digital requires organizations to open up their digital platforms for co-innovation and co-creation. These networked ecosystems provide not only the foundation for such innovation but also a platform for value exchange. While trading networks and innovation communities can provide

standalone options, digital leaders must incorporate these elements into the design of their future platforms in order to gain digital scale.

These next-generation platforms are changing the way we look at technologies. But we can't throw away the existing technologies. They're there, but we build layers into each one of them. So as we moved away from analog systems, we built systems of transaction. As we built systems of transactions, we built engagement layers on top. As we build experiential systems, we're going to connect to those engagement layers. And ultimately, as we build mass personalization at scale, these systems are going to connect into the other layers. There are five layers of getting into digital, and this is really how we apply these new technologies to existing infrastructure in order to be successful.

4. Move to Data-Driven Decisions

The fourth step in moving into the digital business world is moving from gut-driven to data-driven decisions. Data is at the heart of this digital transformation. Every touchpoint, every click, every interaction provides us with digital exhaust that's rich in context. The goal is to move from right-time information overload to real-time contextual relevancy. Organizations need relevancy delivered in real time. This is asking the right questions. This is anticipating future behavior. The goal is to move from data to decisions, and every bit of data flows into upstream and downstream information flows, aligned with business processes. These information flows then provide the foundation for the patterns that provide insight. That business insight then enables people to make fact-based decisions. Serving up the next-best action is the foundation of building these data-driven decisions.

To make those data-driven decisions, we've got to learn to ask what the question really is. There's a lot of hype around big data. It's getting ridiculous. But in fact, when we take a survey of the experts, we get a ton of definitions of what big data is. Some folks see big data as large data sets and data warehouses and operational data sources. Others see big data as a code word for analytics and business intelligence. Some people see the output of big data as infographics or the hardware behind the support of big data. There are other folks that are saying, "Wow, it's intelligence, it's smart, it's going to save and cure everything!" That's not true.

What's the answer? Big data is really about how to ask the right questions. You have to start each project or each solution or each initiative by asking, "What are the questions that need to be asked? What are the answers that will help us move from data to decisions? Can we shift insight into action? How do we tie this information back to a business process? Who needs this information at what right time? And how often should this information be updated, delivered, and shared?"

Moving away from gut-driven toward data-driven decisions is about making choices with an eye toward the future, not rehashing the past. The history in moving from data decisions has been littered with lots of failed technologies. The failure of data warehouses to provide real-time data led to the creation of data marts. Data marts failed to provide complete and updated and comprehensive views, so we moved to business intelligence to access insight. Yet none of this addressed the issues. A movement to master data management helped, but the lack of a central repository of information never got us there. Over the past twenty years, we saw a complete cycle repeat itself. People spent tons of money trying to solve the technology problem with new technologies, yet we still didn't address the key part. So what is it? It's really about getting to the right questions. We have to address the key issue. How can organizations make the right decision? How can you help a leader solve a problem? Business questions remain unanswered, despite all this investment in technology. People are building reports and views and charts, but we have to ask the right questions instead of seeking the right answers. The big shift is about moving from gut to data decisions, and this transformation is in thinking and is not easy to achieve.

5. Co-Create and Co-Innovate with New Partners

Next, we've got to co-create and co-innovate with new partners. No company can succeed on its own. We know that. But in digital transformation, there are ecosystems of co-creation and co-innovation. Organizations can participate in a number of industry consortia and also create their own ecosystem aligned around their organization's self-interest. In many scenarios, an ecosystem doesn't exist, but market-leading and fast-follower vendors, suppliers, and customers are going to come together to solve their problems.

This co-creation and co-innovation is important. Advisers recommend areas for business impact and deliver larger perspectives and trusted advice. Yet, at a higher level, innovators inspire game-changing transformation, conceive and design innovation, and apply disruptive forces—and they lead, too. At the highest level are the creators, who build new technologies in IP for the marketplace. These can be software, products, or even information services, but co-creation becomes supremely important as organizations learn to partner. And partnering in a digital world requires a certain level of discipline that doesn't always exist out there. That's because the way you co-innovate and co-create today, you have to assume that a partnership only works when you realize what you are *not* going to do. You can't partner with anybody if you can't tell him what you're not going to do, because he doesn't know how he can help you without competing with you. It takes a new level of sophistication in this digital business transformation to think about partnerships.

You also partner on different levels. There's product-level alignment. There's sales alignment. There is service- and support-level alignment. And there's ecosystem alignment. And in product alignment, what you want to do is spend a lot of time thinking about what products you're not going to build and how you and your partner can complement each other. It's a very tough decision—especially agreeing on what *not* to do. But if you understand which products

DISRUPTING DIGITAL BUSINESS

you're not going to build, you give people opportunities to build them so that you can focus on what you do best. And that becomes important for co-innovation and co-creation.

On the sales front, you want to make sure that teams are aligned to sell things and that they're incentivized to work together. You don't want to be competing against your partner. You don't want to be underbid by your partner when it doesn't make sense. And so the sales alignment is important. Putting territories together is important. Making sure that they're cross-funded is important.

And then there's service and support. Who's responsible when something breaks? How do you coordinate that? You don't want customers to have a completely broken, fragmented, isolated experience. What you want them to do is have a unified experience. So who handles the first-level support calls? Who handles the second-level support calls? What happens if something breaks? How do you coordinate? Do you have access to each other's systems?

The last piece revolves around ecosystems. The big questions on the ecosystem side are, How do you support each other in the marketplace? How do you bring partners together? How do you form alliances? How do you bring other people into consortiums? And when you have the answers to these questions, you're set for co-innovation and co-creation.

Right now, the existing leadership in most organizations is ill-equipped to drive the change. As a consequence, we've seen the emergence of chief digital officers, which is important for the new age of digital business. People think, "Do we need a CIO? Do we need a CMO? Should the CTO take over digital? Chief digital officers can come from different areas. But we need leaders who are enabled to solve the digital business problems. And the path forward is going to involve a multidisciplinary approach, so the skill sets required for this digital age have got to be infused throughout the executive ranks, in the organization's DNA. We need skills behind digital business transformation that require those tasked with digital leadership to do a few things. These leaders must be able to translate analog business into digital business. This effort is going to require more than adopting a technology or a process. We have to rethink the core business models, those that move from promoting products and services to keeping promises and meeting outcomes. We need to manage this world of trust and radical transparency. Success requires more than fluffy statements about open leadership. The power belongs in building relationships in the personal corporate networks. Leaders have to expect business to move from real time to right time.

Remember: the goal is to develop an authentic business brand. The organization has to ask itself what the company would be like if it were a person. Digital leaders have to think about this every day and then reflect that on customers, employees, partners, and suppliers. The goal is to identify the technologies that will disrupt the business model, so that we get the transformational change. Organizations of all kinds—not just digital media brands—must embrace a central champion who ensures that the digital business principles and policies are in harmony with the organization's overall strategy. The era of the chief digital officer and the digital-enabled CXO is here. Digital leadership is important, and digitally transformed organizations do differentiate themselves with higher margins, greater market share, increased brand relevancy and massive scale. And this is where we want to go as we live and work in this era of digital business.

INDEX

Accenture, 143
access
  argument against paywalls
    and, 138
  to information in next-
    generation platforms, 115,
    121, 165, 168
  as a nonmonetary incentive,
    65, 128–129, 137
  versus ownership of
    information, 160
accountability and trust, 74–75,
  87, 88
Airbus, 28, 29
airline industry, 27–28
Amazon Mechanical Turk, 121
Anderson, Chris, 135
Angie's List, 120
Apple
  flash networks and, 122
  impact on existing business
    models, 25–26
  music business model
    innovation, 24–25
Atlassian, 136, 137
augmented humanity
  designing new experiences
    and, 148, 151

self-learning and, 100, 101,
  102–103, 160
authenticity
  contextual relationships and,
    45–46
  digital artisans and, 153
  digital data exhaust and, 45, 77
  early adopters and, 147
  keeping brand promises and,
    5–6
  requirement to be earned, 72,
    79–80
  sense and respond and, 37, 38
  trust and transparency and,
    71–72, 81, 83, 84, 158

Beck, Glenn, 83
big data business models, 4, 144,
  149–150, 157, 164–165
Bitcoin
  avoidance of a central
    authority, 84–85
  erosion of trust in, 87–88
  premise of, 84
  self-management basis, 85–86
  trust factors applied by,
    86–87

ACKNOWLEDGMENTS

A half-century ago, a man and a woman from Taiwan boarded separate planes to America to pursue their dreams of studying abroad. Each knew that the other was heading to the United States, but they didn't know each other well. In fact, they had met only once through a mutual friend.

The woman arrived early in 1968 to earn a master's degree in specialized education. She had received a scholarship to Northeast Missouri State University and saw the move to the United States as an opportunity to expand her professional career. She had intended to make the journey a year earlier but delayed her trip as she awaited the passing of her mother. She was a city girl at heart but braved the challenges of a new world and those harsh Midwest winters.

The man had come to America in the fall of 1968 with fifty dollars, a full scholarship, and a half-full suitcase to pursue a master's degree in chemical engineering at Montana State University. He bought a ticket to San Francisco, where his older brother lived, thinking it was close to Bozeman, Montana, despite the vastness of the United States. After pooling some money from some kind-hearted acquaintances, he got on a Greyhound bus and finally arrived in Bozeman. Unfortunately, he had come a few weeks before classes started and had no place to live. He found some generous students who took him in and helped him assimilate. He would eventually continue on with school and earn a PhD. Then he graduated into a tough job market during the oil crisis of the 1970s.

By writing incredible letters about what their future together would be like and what they could accomplish together, the man persuaded the woman to come to Bozeman upon graduation. She was the backbone of inspiration that helped him get through his PhD. Through the generosity of the American society at that time and many friends along the way, they eventually settled in Allentown, Pennsylvania, and worked their way into the American dream.

My brother Rex and I are the beneficiaries of this quintessential American story. During the past forty years, our parents managed to impart to us their values of hard work, pursuit of the American dream, and a shared sacrifice to make life better for the next generation. It's this foundation that enables me to share my point of view.

As I thought about who I wanted to dedicate this book to, I knew it had to be my parents. They are pioneers in their own right, and without their selfless love and dedication, I would not be here today. Their endless patience for my crazy ideas and their support of the interesting twists in my life journey can never be repaid in this lifetime but only paid forward to my children, loved ones, and friends.

Writing a book was not something I could have imagined doing in my childhood. I set out to be a scientist or inventor or physician. Somehow, I found myself spending less time with numbers and more time with simplifying abstract concepts, engaging in design, and improving my writing. Life does provide some unexpected turns, but each experience builds upon the others.

There are many folks I do want to thank for helping this book become a reality. My wife, Tina, has put up with each of my crazy ideas for more than twenty-three years. And I've had a ton of them. I also want to thank our kids, Nathan and Stephanie, for patiently standing by as they wondered what Dad was up to with late-night writing sessions, research, and massive travel. The time with them can't be made up, but I do miss them a lot when I'm away. Hopefully it will all make sense to them one day.

When you think about your foundation and your core, you start with those teachers and other educators who inspired you. I do want to thank some inspirational teachers, such as Chuck Tannery from Spring House Junior High, whose passion for English and public speaking left a lasting impression on me regarding how to tell a story. Sister Mary Francis from Allentown Central Catholic High School provided encouragement to pursue the sciences with rigor, serving as a champion of support for my high school Westinghouse Science Talent Search.

Careerwise, the many mentors along the way include Jim Johns and Greg Finnegan at Johns Hopkins Hospital, who recognized early on that I was a disruptor but taught me how to channel that hyperactivity and the impatience of youth into something more fitting for the corporate world. Peggy Sawyer, then at Ernst & Young, was an encouraging force as we went through the SAP journey of learning how to configure complex German software. She taught me how to work hard, play hard, and navigate complex politics. Reza Soudagar at Oracle helped me develop a Silicon Valley big-company approach to building products and how to deal with different leadership styles and crazy politics.

Love Goel, then CEO of Personify, showed me how to think big and aim for the art of the possible. I thank John Ragsdale and Merv Adrian at Forrester Research for believing in me and giving me a start in this wonderful industry. Paul Hamerman helped me understand what the role of an industry analyst was. Meanwhile, my research director, Sharyn Leaver, gave me enough latitude to push the envelope in how industry research could be conducted and what it meant to innovate in the research field and build a personal brand.

The company I founded, Constellation Research, has entered its fourth year of business, and I'm very thankful for a great team. None of this would be possible without our COO, Dennis Kanemitsu, and our director of operations, Elaine Chen, who have held down the fort as I've struggled to take any available time slot to write. A key source of inspiration has been our three-hundred-plus clients roster. Because we are a Silicon Valley–based research firm, many of the book's concepts have come from working with clients who are disrupting digital business. Those individual points have helped us plot the trends that have led to this digital business revolution.

In addition, I have had the good fortune of many mentors along the way. Paul Greenberg, often known as the

Godfather of CRM, has provided great mentorship and guidance on not only writing this book, but also on how to grow a personal brand and company. Erin Kinikin, who rejected my application to Forrester three times before accepting it (well, she was on vacation when they hired me) and is now a trusted adviser, has been invaluable in providing perspective on research focus and how to grow analysts. Esteban Kolsky, a dear friend, has been a great resource in battle testing ideas in this digital disruption space. And my brother Rex, who knows me well enough to apply some sanity to my chaos on a regular basis.

As I wrote this book, there were many other folks who played a key role. I have to thank Kathleen Carr at Harvard Business Review Press, who reached out to me in October 2010 and surprised me with the initial offer. Special thanks go out to Kevin Smokler, my classmate at Johns Hopkins, who helped me understand how to tell the story in a conversational approach. In fact, his uncanny ability to synthesize a story led to many great suggestions and style techniques used throughout the text. His knowledge of the book industry helped provide insights into the process.

I also want to thank Justin Fox, my initial editor at Harvard Business Review Press, for putting up with the three years it took a draft in place. He helped me relearn how to write in the first person after years of having my writing style at Forrester beat out of me into a third-person approach. Finally, I have to thank Tim Sullivan, my current editor, for giving me the final push and encouragement to complete this book four years from its initial concept. There were times I probably would have given up, but his patience with me and my chaotic schedule, his ability to pull my thoughts into words, and his insightful ability to tell the story have made this book what it is.

As you read this book, understand that I have you to thank for taking the time to read these thoughts. I encourage you to reach out to me on e-mail, LinkedIn, or in the Twittersphere. I want to know your point of view and if this book has given you a different perspective on what your art of the possible can be. I truly appreciate you picking this book up. Please set forth and go disrupt digital business!

ABOUT THE AUTHOR

R "RAY" WANG is the Principal Analyst, Founder, and Chairman of Silicon Valley–based Constellation Research, Inc. He's also the author of the popular enterprise software blog *A Software Insider's Point of View*. With tens of millions of page views a year, his blog provides insight into how disruptive technologies and new business models impact the enterprise. Prior to founding Constellation, Wang was a founding partner and research analyst for enterprise strategy at Altimeter Group and one of the top analysts at Forrester Research for business and IT strategy. He has held executive roles in product, marketing, strategy, and consulting at companies such as Forrester Research, Oracle, PeopleSoft, Deloitte, Ernst & Young, and Johns Hopkins Hospital. He's also been a CMO at Personify Inc, a web-analytics software start-up valued at $500M during the internet boom.

A background in emerging business and technology trends, digital business model transformation, enterprise apps strategy, technology selection, and contract negotiations enables Wang to provide clients and readers with a bridge between business leadership and technology adoption. Buyers seek his research in future trends and disruptive technologies and value his insights into the business processes, business models, and organizational design required for successful adoption.

Wang is a highly sought-after thought leader and keynote speaker. His dynamic speaking style brings energy and enthusiasm to a range of topics, from business strategy to management and leadership. Wang tailors his presentations to intimate audiences in boardrooms as well as to the tens of thousands of listeners who tune in to his live-broadcast keynotes.

Wang's works, quotes, and interviews can be found in media such as *Harvard Business Review,* the *Wall Street Journal, Bloomberg BusinessWeek, Fortune, Inc.,* the Associated Press, *CIO Magazine, InformationWeek, Computer-World, Financial Times, eWeek, CRM Magazine, IDG News Service, ZDNet, TechTarget,* and *Managing Automation.* Wang has also been featured on major TV news outlets, such as CNBC and Bloomberg.

In 2008, 2009, and 2014 Wang was recognized by the prestigious Institute of Industry Analyst Relations (IIAR) as the Analyst of the Year, and in 2009 he was recognized as one of the most important analysts for Enterprise, SMB, and Software. In 2009, *A Software Insider's Point of View* was listed in the top twenty of Jonny Bentwood's *Techno-babble 2.0*'s Top Industry Analyst Blogs. In 2010, Wang was listed as one of the Top Five Analyst Tweeters in Edelman's Telecoms TweetLevel Index, recorded as part of the ARInsights Power 100 List of Industry Analysts, and named one of the top Influential Leaders by *CRM Magazine* as part of its 2010 Market Awards.

Wang is a Taiwanese American residing in the Silicon Valley with his wife and two children.